"Jody Dean's approach to the topic of [...] of your work and ministry is a much-needed [...] I wish I'd had available to me years ago. Practical, insightful, and [...] describe this new work. Read this book, and learn from a great leader."

**—Ken Braddy**, director of Sunday school and network
partnerships, Lifeway Christian Resources

"Jody Dean's *Managing the Ministry* serves as a guide to help leaders navigate organizational leadership challenges of church ministry. My thirty-year journey of pastoral experience and twelve years as a professor at a Baptist university have provided both a practical and an academic perspective. Not only is this work valuable for academic training, but it also serves as a daily leadership reference for those in ministry. Dean helps the reader navigate the organizational challenges inherent to ministry while also weaving in scriptural support and personal stories that make the book enjoyable to read. I am personally grateful for Jody's commitment to helping leaders during a time when church health is so crucial."

**—T. Brett Golson**, vice president of spiritual development
and church relations and professor of religion, William Carey
University

"Ministers are often not prepared to be ministry managers. Yet, dealing with budgets, personnel, buildings, and legal issues is part of day-to-day ministry leadership. This book offers sound management counsel, in language and context ministers understand, to help bridge the training gap and prepare ministers to be better managers. Seminaries need a textbook like this, and churches need a guidebook like this. Use this tool to improve your ministry by becoming a better manager."

**—Jeff Iorg**, president, Gateway Seminary

"Whether you are a seminary student or an experienced local church minister, this book will provide a practical framework for church administration. It is an excellent guide for helping you manage ministry in our rapidly changing world. It is not a technical 'how to' manual but exposes you to vital issues the local church must address in its context."

**—David Jeffreys**, executive vice president and chief operating
officer, Louisiana Christian University

"One of the most-needed but often most-neglected aspects of ministry training is in how to lead a church through administrative oversight. *Managing the Ministry* addresses this need. Jody Dean has provided a biblically grounded and practically focused resource for those who desire their administrative leadership to be more than managing daily operations. This book is intended for those who want to lead ministry and not simply manage programs. Jody rightly focuses on management as leadership, blending the best of biblical leadership expressed in gospel ministry. And Jody rightly keeps the focus on the true goal of management: leading God's people into deeper relationships with and more faithful service to the living God. I highly recommend this excellent book to anyone who desires to learn how to lead a ministry or to improve their leadership in their current ministry."

> —**R. Stanton Norman**, president, Williams Baptist University

"Every gospel ministry leader will be involved in administration in some way. It's an intrinsic part of shepherding people in Christ's church. However, not all approach it with the kingdom demeanor it demands. My friend Jody Dean brings practical experience, diligent research, and deep spirituality to the conversation to help us navigate this task in a way that resembles the leadership of King David: 'He shepherded them with a pure heart and guided them with his skillful hands' (Ps 78:72)."

> —**Jim Shaddix**, W. A. Criswell Professor of Expository Preaching
> and senior fellow, Center for Preaching and Pastoral Leadership,
> Southeastern Baptist Theological Seminary

"Recent events have highlighted the incredible need for faithful and competent leaders to guide our churches especially in an era when church business and organizational practices are held rightly to the high standard of biblical integrity. Training resources like *Managing the Ministry* are invaluable to the process of equipping the best leaders for these times."

> —**Chris Shirley**, dean, Jack D. Terry School of Educational
> Ministries, Southwestern Baptist Theological Seminary

# Managing
# the Ministry

# Managing the Ministry

*A Practical Guide to*
*Church Administration*

# Jody Dean

ACADEMIC
BRENTWOOD, TENNESSEE

# Contents

## Part 3:
## Organizational Coaching

# Introduction

Each of us can be a leader. We can delegate our work and grant others the ability to complete a task. Leaders desire to multiply their work through others. This book is an encouragement for enhancing the management and administration of your ministry. Through stories embedded into the chapters, you will be encouraged that you are not alone in this work. We have countless colleagues every week working in churches to make his name known. This practical guide will cover many topics designed to cause you to ponder administration through the lens of your ministry. You may be prompted to consider an area that you are doing well, or another topic may generate ideas for tweaks that should be made in your organization. Maybe something you read will cause you to pause and pray. Each week the administration of our ministries is managed, but we are never perfect when executing the details. We deal with people, property, processes, and programs as we strive to execute the work well.

If you picked up this book, then chances are you desire to learn more about church administration or struggle with an area in your ministry and desire to improve. This book is intended to be a resource for you and your church to be able to tackle the administrative issues of ministry. You will find three sections designed around three components of church administration. The first section will guide you through the five key foundational areas of ministry management. In the second section, you will be guided through areas of challenges with considerations for your ministry. The last section is focused on administrative opportunities that can enhance your work through the local church. Coaching through these opportunities will have a great impact on managing the work well. When this approach is taken, many aspects of ministry can move forward in ways that are more productive, collaborative, or engaging in the church.

You may have various people in your church that would benefit from working through this resource together and discussing how it applies to your setting. Another option is to read with your mentor in ministry or a group of ministry leaders from within or outside your local church. This book is designed in a way that enables you to skim for chapters that cover topics that directly relate to your needs.

One of the specific gifts listed in Scripture along with pastors, teachers, or evangelists is the gift of administration (1 Cor 12:28, ESV). We find that throughout Scripture, God provided examples of administration among his people and for his church. Some have this gift naturally, but others might find themselves struggling in this area. This book was written for all of you, no matter what your giftings may be. As you read, pray that your mind will be opened to principles and processes that will benefit you as you manage the church from your position of responsibility.

# PART 1:

# ORGANIZATIONAL FOUNDATIONS

A strong foundation is vital to building and managing any structure. When constructing buildings in the Gulf South, special care must be taken to calculate foundations based on the water levels within the ground that determine how deep to drive pilings into the earth. The local church makes similar considerations to the foundational aspects of ministry. Churches need a strong organizational foundation to navigate the challenges of ministry in the twenty-first century. People who experienced the dawn of this century were greeted with tremendous anxiety over Y2K and what that year's calibration might do to computer systems, including banking systems worldwide. Still, New Year's Eve came and went, and the world continued to spin without the impending digital crisis. This began a century that has provided people with increased anxiety in the first three decades, and the events keep coming.

The terrorist attacks of 9/11 wreaked havoc through highjacked airplanes. A recession caused people to panic about their financial futures. The racial divide has been further exposed through riots and protests erupting across the nation. Politics has divided families, offices, and churches as conversational topics have become controversial. The COVID-19 pandemic changed the lives of the world population in just a few months. As war and unrest play out worldwide, financial banking concerns and political divides have the usual ebb and flow in our rhythm of life and ministry.

The challenges, however, should not outweigh the positives we also see in ministry. We have more adults than ever to minister in the church. The intergenerational possibilities for ministry are endless. Although the challenges seem never ending, there are new opportunities for the church. People have gifts and need to be equipped to serve. The property as an asset needs to be maintained and managed. Finances provide the resources necessary to execute ministry. Programming needs to run smoothly. Processes are increasing as society becomes more complex. This section of chapters will explore these challenges and opportunities for organizational management in the church.

# Chapter 1:

# People Development and Management

On any given week, you can look out into the congregation and see various ages, life experiences, and giftedness for ministry among the faces of the church. We cannot accomplish the ministry that we are called to without people. People are the key to getting the gospel to the next generation. As we consider administration, we must consider the human component of our organization. Most of you reading this book serve in the local church in some capacity. You are probably reading this book because you hope to improve the organizational leadership within your church. In discussing this topic, we begin with human resource management as an essential element of organizing people to accomplish the work of ministry. Leading people has always been a challenge, even as far back as the lives of Noah or Moses. Human resources can be laborious and often come with headaches.

Throughout the Bible, we see examples of people's trials that remind us of modern human resource challenges. First, we observe Moses's leadership in Exodus 18. He managed people's issues while trying to lead them through the ebb and flow of seeking the Promised Land after being released from slavery in Egypt. The challenge of managing people's problems, disputes, and daily needs was overwhelming. Moses and his father-in-law stepped in and created a pathway of dividing and working with the people in a hierarchical leadership system with divisions of thousands to hundreds to tens, making the people's issues more manageable. In 1 Samuel 17, David was not perceived as a leader but challenged the odds and proved he was the man needed against Goliath. The people already had hundreds of warriors present at the battle, but a young shepherd boy was utilized to deliver the victory. We like an underdog story in leadership, such as David who overcame the odds and slayed the giant. As you read the Old Testament, you continue to encounter people that addressed people's challenges in order to lead.

In the New Testament, we see examples such as John the Baptist who led through preparing the way for Jesus and continued to overcome the odds to proclaim the truth. [1] Jesus, at a young age, engaged with the leadership at the temple and continued to lead people during his earthly ministry.[2] Though imperfect, the disciples endured to the end by proclaiming the gospel to the next generation and birthing the early church. Jesus still encountered leadership challenges among the disciples as they desired to know how they ranked from least to greatest. He continued to experience leaders who wanted to challenge his theology, beliefs, and identity, ultimately leading to the cross. In the early church, we encounter a leader named Paul, who wrote many letters to churches that had various divisions and challenges. Hopefully, you find some encouragement through the generations of church leaders who walked faithfully with God. They navigated staffing, divisions, and questions from the people so that the mission never stopped. In your church, the challenges with staff and volunteers will be an ongoing area to cultivate a team mindset and find ways to allow people to utilize their time, gifts, and experiences to serve through the church.

Administration is one of the gifts listed in the New Testament.[3] Hence, administering the work is crucial in the church with pastors, ministers, directors, support staff, and lay leaders. Personnel is an aspect that impacts any church size. Each congregation has volunteers that agree to serve in a position with a given responsibility and then are put into service to fulfill that commitment for a period of time.

---

[1] John 3:22–36.
[2] Luke 2:41–52.
[3] 1 Cor 12:28 (ESV).

A vetting process should be followed, responsibilities identified, and training conducted to accomplish the work. People are needed to keep everything moving forward in advancing the work. Without people, all ministries within the local church would stop since God decided to use people as the means to get the gospel from one generation of believers to the next. The command is simple for the people: "Go, therefore, and make disciples of all nations, baptizing them in the name of the Father and of the Son and of the Holy Spirit, teaching them to observe everything I have commanded you. And remember, I am with you always, to the end of the age."[4] People were and still are the plan created by God to pass the gospel to the nations. As we seek to execute this mission, challenges with people arise in our churches. Our properties and programs need alignment with the mission as each aspect is staffed with volunteers, paid support, and paid ministerial oversight.

Management is vital in the church because people matter, and each family has needs to fulfill. Moblilizing people to meet expectations, the church should utilize systems, tools, and other resources for effective administration. Charles Tidwell provided a definition of church administration in a different generation of church leadership that remains relevant to ponder today:

> Church administration is the leadership which equips the church to be the church and do the work of the church. It is the guidance provided by church leaders as they lead the church to use its spiritual, human, physical, and financial resources to move the church toward reaching its objectives and fulfilling its intended purpose. It is enabling the children of God who comprise the church to become and to do what they can become and do, by God's grace.[5]

Equipping people to become who God has called them to be should always remain in focus through church ministry leadership.

As you ponder people and ministry, you can utilize administrative mapping to determine how many people are needed to staff the work. Identify each ministry and how many unique volunteers are needed. Map the weekly and monthly forecast for age-graded ministry, worship, discipleship, missions, committees, leadership, and staff

---

[4] Matt 28:19–20.
[5] Charles A. Tidwell, *Church Administration: Effective Leadership for Ministry* (Nashville: Broadman, 1985), 27.

assignments. Then, you can determine between the unique ministries and scheduled activities the amount of people it will take to accomplish the work through your church based on how it is currently structured. You can then access the positions that require paid leadership, those that need volunteer oversight, and those that a volunteer can administer.

An organizational map can feel daunting if your ministry has been like mine, primarily in existing, established churches. As you conduct organizational mapping, you may find committees whose functions remain unclear, but you fill vacancies for their committee each year. Some of your committees need to pivot to become less formal ministry teams. You may even have committees that could be eliminated because the days of their usefulness in the mission have been exhausted. Some areas of ministry might exist that you were not aware of or did not consider a ministry of your church. Administrative mapping, then, produces a clear view of the total positions of service in your church, including teachers, committees, deacons, ministry teams, and assigned volunteers.

The second phase of mapping the organization requires the people to be scheduled. Who do you need to accomplish the work of your church or ministry and when are they required? You may have volunteers who serve for extended periods of time on the first impressions team or media team. Some volunteer roles are weekly, some are monthly, and others rotate based on the needs of your ministry. Volunteers may teach a small group, sing in the choir, or play the drums in the praise team. The administrative task of staffing the organization is an ongoing endeavor, and each church will have nuances to its schedule, ministries, and staffing needs. Identifying the people needed and scheduling them into your system will help you complete an administrative map of the people necessary to accomplish the planned work of the church.

Volunteer needs must be identified and specific instructions should be given to each volunteer. A small group leader, for example, should know the time of the meeting, place of meeting, and curriculum used. A committee needs to know when it meets, how often, expectations and responsibilities, and location and time of the meetings. This may sound simple, but many volunteers must be given clear instructions when hired or recruited. Leaders who are familiar with the routine of filling vacancies each year tend to expect other people to understand the process and the needs. When asked, it is often assumed that the responsibilities and functions are expected but only sometimes communicated.

Volunteers need to know the importance of the task they are being given. People want to respond to a compelling vision or need that is apparent. If a leader explains why a position is needed, people can determine if it is a wise stewardship of their talents. The volunteer wants these questions answered, but the paid support staff and ministerial staff need them answered. Later in the book, we will discuss financial and time stewardship. These two aspects are easy to quantify, but talent stewardship is more complicated as people serve throughout their week at home with their families, at the office, at church, at school, or in the community. The church should help cultivate talent stewardship through explaining why a person is needed in a specific position.

## Organizational Management Considerations for Staffing

Your organization's staffing levels need to be identified, and each organization must consider how it assigns staff roles. There are seven classifications that most churches will deal with in their ministry:

| | |
|---|---|
| VM: | volunteer with minors |
| VNM: | volunteer without minor clearance |
| PTSS: | part-time support staff |
| FTSS: | full-time support staff |
| PTM: | co-vocational ministerial staff |
| FTM: | full-time ministerial staff |
| C: | contract staff |

Another consideration for staffing relates to the church office. The chapter on Organizational Processes will cover many aspects of the staff and church office. A few areas that need to be considered for all people that work in the organization as a volunteer or paid are as follows.

## *Moral Conduct for Staff*

News outlets over the years have reported on ministers, staff, and volunteers that have had moral failures and committed sinful acts, involving both minors and adults in the church. As allegations have been raised, many churches have been left to figure out how the failure or sinful act occurred. Recent tragedies such as these have caused many to question their faith and relationship with the church. Staff and volunteers need accountability processes and safeguards. Satan is actively pursuing those he can tempt toward evil, thus the people of God must be aware that even in the church with good people, sinful things happen.[6] One component of being a shepherd is to protect the flock from threats inside and outside the church. Much time could be spent discussing past tragedies and failures in church leadership, but the administrator must focus on the present and plan for the future. How do you safeguard the people entrusted to your care from the moral failures of staff and volunteers in the church? We will discuss common risk factors in ministry in chapter nine. Staff and volunteers are employed to serve in leadership roles with a position description and a challenge to live for Christ. The administrative perspective causes us to consider the person's character and how to support them with moral accountability when so many sinful moral failures begin in private, often through a smartphone or website.

## Policies for Staff

Often, in the human resource space, a policy is written in reaction to a problem or a specific issue that has happened in the past. A later chapter is dedicated to policy and procedures, but it is an aspect that needs clarity for all who are employed in various ways in the organization. The intent when policies are created is that supervisors will enforce the policies evenly for all staff without bias. A reaction to an issue is not the best environment to establish policy because the tendency is often overcorrection. As leaders, we should seek wise counsel and understand the best approaches to guide our church *ethos* and create staff policies that maintain the vision and mission of the church with a biblical foundation while providing a framework for clear accountability in which the staff operates each week.

## Hiring Process of Staff

In the nineteen-seventies, the three prescribed areas for considering a person for staff were recruiting, screening, and placing.[7] Although

---

[6] 1 Pet 5:8.
[7] Leonard E. Wedel, *Church Staff Administration* (Nashville: Broadman, 1978), 11.

these three areas have changed over the years, the process is still simple. An application process is utilized to screen applicants and obtain permission to conduct background checks and screenings like drug tests and review references. Hiring the wrong fit for the organization, from a volunteer to a pastor, can cause many long-term challenges. You have probably heard of the concept where the team members are arranged to the ideal seat on the bus. This allows everyone to serve in a place that fits their unique skill set and becomes more productive for the organization. A wrong fit can challenge relationships, drain resources, or divide people. The negatives can be overcome but usually result in the loss of church members. Here are just a few examples: (1) a student pastor that is insubordinate and hard to get along with in the office but is beloved and interacts differently with students, families, and the larger congregation; or (2) a volunteer who is drama-prone but expects to be on the praise team rotation more than others. These are just two examples where those causing issues have a following and can persuade or divide the people and leave ministers in situations where they cannot divulge the total picture of the problem.

## Compensation for Staff

Money is one of those areas where people have many emotions regarding the job. In a church, people must understand that some are volunteers and we cannot do the work without their service to the Lord. In addition, people must realize that various compensation levels exist based on the type of position, skills required, education, and experience. The senior pastor is the highest compensated in almost all churches. The New Testament discusses the need to treat those in ministry service well and provide for their needs. As we have support staff from the office, facility, and other types of employment, we begin to navigate how to treat those that serve in a paid staff role that supports the organizational work but is not considered ministerial or pastoral staff.

When a person is hired, they choose to accept the terms of employment with job description expectations and compensation offered. The employee has some responsibility if they develop a negative attitude toward compensation provided and accepted, whether a pastor, minister, or staff member. Although volunteers do not receive direct compensation, they may still have access to what some might label as perks. For example, some perks may include a resource room, copier, computer access, or memberships to resources for their position. They may attend conferences or utilize other church resources that could be seen as benefits, which would be indirect compensation.

## Training for Staff

By the time the sun sets on a person's season of service, the landscape has changed. Thus, training is necessary to adapt to new developments. The congregation, community, and culture continue to change as people serve; therefore, the needs also morph. For this reason, ongoing training is necessary for those who wish to continue excelling in their areas of responsibility. People do not enjoy serving in a position when the knowledge to execute their function is lacking or expectations are unclear. A call center where someone cannot help the person because they do not have enough information or training is as frustrating for the employee as the customer calling for assistance. The church can be the same when we do not train people for their role in the church.

## Termination, Suspension, Discipline for Staff

Ministry is challenging when a person who serves in leadership has personal, professional, or ministry issues that are below the standard outlined in God's Word and stated by the church's expectations for leaders. Over time in American culture, the word *discipline* has grown to have negative connotations, but it does have a redemptive lens from Scripture. The discipline of the Lord is not pleasant, but as we observe the people of Israel struggling to follow God without turning to sin, we understand the challenges in our churches. We still have a rebellious heart with desires and temptations that are distorted or evil when not placed under the lordship of Christ. A discipline process for theft, sexual misconduct, and any form of misconduct with a minor should lead to the immediate termination of employment. I would never recommend separation or discipline rather than termination if any person in leadership goes against the qualifications of the office they hold for an elder, teacher, or deacon. However, not all issues warrant termination. Sometimes, a person has an undeveloped work ethic that needs to be nurtured toward a healthy level of investment. Many areas are difficult to navigate with leaders, especially concerning social media, alcohol, and even medical marijuana. These have become areas of concern that various generations view differently in the church.

These six areas will never be flawless in an organization because we deal with people. Being aware that a plan is needed for these aspects as you deal with all designations of an employee will help limit future frustration. Most churches have problems because there is no developed process or because people try to find shortcuts. *Stewardship* is a word that is often used in association to finances but can be applied to people as well. Individual talents and time are assets that sometimes receive less thought, plans, or goal settings. Managing talent often brings thoughts of college or pro athletes or your favorite actor or artist; however, shift your thinking toward your ministry and ponder the talent you have been blessed to work with. If you went to a website of a premier agency that manages talent, you would find a portfolio of clients that use that service for managing their work. I have done this many times to book an artist for an event at church. The agencies should prioritize the artists', personalities', or athletes' best interests when negotiating on their behalf. The struggle in ministry is that, besides paid staff, we manage a large group of volunteers through the various ministries and events we administer each year.

Managing talent is vital. In a few chapters, we will discuss the workforce and aspects that contribute to their effectiveness. You do not want to mismanage the talent in your church; however, you can find yourself busy and not give full attention to others' needs and skills, thus mismanaging people's ability to contribute fully to the work. As you consider talent, it may help them understand their spiritual gifts, personalities, and leadership styles. Many resources exist to help people see the indicators of their skills and abilities. These can help, but as we grow and mature in a relationship with Christ, people must also understand that these indicators can change over time.

The goal would be for our staff or volunteers never to think their ministry and service to the Lord is the end of the road for their lives. *Creative Church Administration* describes congregation values as expressed by the people, which when explored could inform creativity for planning, decision-making, and administration in the congregation. A few questions should be asked to discover the values: "In your congregation, what are the values expressed, creativity or verbal skills? Tradition or innovation? Ministry or Money? Representation of the optimum number of groups and organizations, or performance? Care of people or care of the property? Responsible, representative church government, or personal satisfaction? Distributing scarce leadership talents fairly among excess needs or encouraging self-motivation?"[8] These questions indicate a lot about a local church and its values and will be instrumental in how you begin to view the organizational management needed to equip people for the work.

A verse that has ministered to me for decades in this regard is found in First Corinthians: "Therefore, my dear brothers and sisters, be steadfast, immovable, always excelling in the Lord's work, because you know that your labor in the Lord is not in vain."[9] As we approach the administrative task of managing our people, the goal should be to help maturing disciples to be steadfast. This unique word of being steadfast in the work means to endure patiently: "A steadfast person is one who is reliable, faithful, and true to the end."[10] The goal in managing the workforce should be to help people be reliable, faithful, and true to their ministerial responsibilities. Being immovable indicates that the people would not waiver but would be solid disciples in the faith. Always excelling suggests that each week the people would be progressing in the work and maturing into who Christ has called each of us to become. To do something in vain, a person is unreliable and self-conceited, but we are called to obedience and not just lip service.[11] When we are serving for the right reasons in ministry, it is in obedience to Christ and not for ourselves.

[8] Lyle E. Schaller and Charles A. Tidwell, *Creative Church Administration* (Nashville: Abingdon, 1975), 17.

[9] 1 Cor 15:58.

[10] *Holman Illustrated Bible Dictionary* (Nashville: B&H, 2003), 1533.

[11] *Holman Illustrated Bible Dictionary*, 1645.

# Chapter 2:

# Property Development and Management

People are an essential asset to any ministry, but church property becomes the second most significant asset to the church. The responsibility of stewarding assets can be challenging. Any building or property of the church is just like the blessing our homes are to us; they must be maintained and cared for. You can drive through an older neighborhood and see beautiful homes maintained well with great landscaping and others that could qualify for an HGTV *Fixer Upper* episode. A church needs to consider the importance of preserving all aspects of its property as part of the mission unto the Lord. An asset that we have should not be buried but nurtured to multiply the overall work. This chapter will unpack the challenges, strategies, and concepts to steward the property you have been blessed with.

Believers have invested in properties in many ways for generations. In the Old Testament, the tabernacle was a sacrifice of time and effort to set up, maintain, and move with the people. The building of the temple was a multiple generational effort that required finances, time, and effort to accomplish. The rebuilding of the temple required the same level of effort. In the New Testament, the people of God move beyond the temple to the house church, which was a personal investment of a family for the community. We still practice this level of personal investment in many ways as we open our homes to ministry through different events and discipleship moments. The family is the key component in this task. Church buildings then became more localized and an effort of the people to build a place to gather for the functions of the church expanded as ministries grew. This is the strategy we see today in many communities worldwide.

Because families have invested time and resources into a property, they feel some ownership of the building. They have provided for the furnishings, usage, and overall maintenance. Fond memories and familial connection also create a desire to care for that property just as they do for their own personal properties. Everyone cares for their property differently. Some people value landscaping, while others think it is an unnecessary expense. Some desire to remodel and refresh the look of their home on the exterior and interior consistently, while others are content to wait until something needs to be fixed or replaced. Leaders must navigate the various perspectives of the people as the property ages and different ministry needs change over time. As you begin to consider your organization, the approach to facilities and the overall property will impact each of the following areas that need a process for managing the property.

An organization must consider the costs of maintaining any facility or property. Another factor is the necessary insurance to cover people, property, programs, and the organization. A facility must be cleaned and maintained regularly, including exterior landscaping services and seasonal items like pressure washing. A facility should be furnished to allow the organization to maximize the usage of the property. The organization then looks at a comprehensive maintenance plan for managing the property. Contract services provide some options but are a separate component for the organization's maintenance needs.

Property impacts the organization's finances due to the ongoing operating and maintenance costs associated with a facility and grounds. A church's budget reflects this level of care, with maintenance, insurance, and utilities comprising a large portion. This resource is maintained each week, which adds supply and labor costs to the organization. The financial component is a challenge for many churches as facilities, and the tithers within, age. Economic downfalls also impact the maintenance costs of labor, supplies, and materials, causing this budget item to become more expensive. The utilities to occupy a building depend on the cost of these services to the church. Electricity, gas, water, and sewage are also factored into the financial impact of a property.

## Furnishing the Church Property

Two main approaches exist when furnishing churches. One is to reflect the home décor of the families of the church through donations. The other is furnishing with commercial décor, which may invoke a school, hospital, or business furnishing style instead of a family living room motif. These considerations may remind you of a church you visited where it was apparent someone with good taste had visited a local furniture store and picked lovely pieces of furniture for the foyer and other sitting areas of the church.

The pandemic brought challenges of disinfecting and caring for the home décor version of furnishing. A commercial furnishing approach can work in any size organization because the kind of furnishing is the question to solve, not the size of the church. Proper church furnishing should look nice, meet the appropriate age use, and reflect wise stewardship. Investing in commercial-grade items that can last and be cared for with wear and tear over time can be challenging for some but may serve the long-term need of churches. As you consider the furnishings be mindful that a facility should be welcoming and provide clear directional signage that allows people to find their way to the places they need to be. The desire to have commercial types of furnishing should not take away the inviting warmth of common areas in the facility. The ongoing challenge is helping people think about outreach and focus on the needs of others and not their own preferences.

## Maintenance Factors

As a home ages, challenges arise because any new home will eventually need a roof, air conditioning unit, stove, or plumbing repair, to name a few. The church facility is, in the same way, an aging structure that will eventually need to be repaired, remodeled, or replaced even with the finest aspects of lighting and seating. Since maintenance is part of an organization's ongoing relationship with its property, a wise steward will develop the best plan possible to care for the property. This plan allows the people to know the needs, become involved, and care for the facility. Stewardship is not to be confused with ownership. At my house, I am to steward the blessing of the home from the Lord. But because I also own the house, I have a responsibility to steward and care for the home. In the church, the people are the stewards, but the organization is the owner.

Sometimes stewardship creeps toward ownership control. My grandparents owned a lake house where their expectations ruled and the rest of the family had little input in how the house was used. Rules are not always accessible or understandable to people, just as I did not appreciate my grandparent's rules. Still, the organization must make rules for the church. One rule we had as kids was to wear a life jacket when swimming in the lake. We did not like the rule, but the adults wanted to keep us safe. We also had to help care for the property, so yard work before swimming or skiing was typical over spring break. Now, think about the church. As we ask our people to help with the church property, it becomes like caring for that second home. This is where the people and the property begin to compete. If property care began to consume too much of the lake time growing up, then we wouldn't even want to go to the lake house anymore. As my grandpa said, "I only work when I get to go." The church's priority with people is to invest in serving toward worship, discipleship, and missions. Thus, we cast a vision of how the property fits within the framework of the work we do which is why we invest the resources of people and finances to care for our properties.

The answer to the church's maintenance plans may not be simply scheduling Saturday workdays. An ongoing maintenance plan that includes replacing old building components, improving the facility, and maintaining a fresh, inviting feel to the space will foster longevity in your property. There will always be challenges to properties that create the need for a remodel project that the congregation will eventually have to navigate. People do not usually get excited about maintenance remodel projects, air conditioning systems, boilers, or roofs but are more inclined to give toward projects in the worship space, student space, or an overall refresh of the interior. Organizations, however, are expected to plan for repairing and replacing items known to have a lifespan of usefulness. A new building is hardly ever the answer to these challenges because more unused space may not be a viable plan for dealing with maintenance. Some people will sell their homes and relocate to avoid a remodel, but most update the home they have.

A new building will have all the modern features, more energy efficient systems, and be inviting to all that come. But eventually, the new building becomes familiar and needs to be maintained. I have enjoyed consulting churches for years in this area. One aspect that has always amazed me is how people refer to buildings over ten or twenty years old as the new gym, new fellowship hall, or new sanctuary. Buildings lose their freshness over time. If you are older, you likely remember when Wal-Mart was not a superstore that included groceries. As demand increased, they built new stores and renovated older ones. You have probably been to a Wal-Mart as they were updating the flooring and paint. Now those stores have moved from taupe to gray to virtual to meet customers' needs. This is just one example of how a building or space will need ongoing cultivation for the current needs of the ministry.

A fresh and inviting space should be achievable for any structure. I have been in houses of many different sizes, ages, and designs for a family visit or ministry event. These types of visits provide a first-hand experience of how diverse people live. Some people have homes ready for an open house while others have homes with a lived-in feel to them. Homes are defined by curb appeal and the inviting environment upon entering the house. I have seen older homes with great curb appeal. I have been in homes that are extremely warm and welcoming. I once had a realtor that would bake cookies twenty minutes before a showing, so it smelled inviting and welcoming to potential home-owners. We must apply this concept as we think about staying fresh in our ministry so that people feel welcomed as they attend.

## Contracting Maintenance

Contracts are an aspect of the property that seminary may not have prepared you for in your ministry. Contracts provide a service from a business and require a legal signature from an approved representative of the organization. Once you enter into the contract, a company's insurance should have your organization on file and provide a copy of their certificate of insurance for you. One type of contract includes on-going services that are needed daily, for example, internet, dumpster rental, or security system. Another type of contract is for service plans that are available as needed or annually, including HVAC maintenance or inspections of fire extinguishers, elevators, or kitchen commercial hoods. Special event contracts could be needed for property rentals, audio/visual equipment for Christmas programs, or inflatables for the kids' back-to-school picnic. Rental agreements are another type of contract for camp retreat centers, equipment rentals, or services like inflatables or a dunking booth. Food service supply, janitorial supply, and other vendor services must be coordinated with staffing and office hours so that the deliveries and items that need servicing or repair can be completed. If you are a smaller staff and decide you will close and leave early because things are slow, then deliveries, vendors, and services must be considered. We will discuss more on coordination later.

## *Janitorial Factors*

As you approach having a clean facility, the big picture of determining your overall weekly need is essential. If the church has two major facility usages per week, then being clean on Sunday and Wednesday is a priority for the janitorial staff. The work must be scheduled weekly so the team knows when a unique event or space is utilized differently than the week before. The church staff should determine the labor hours needed for tasks to plan the workload. How many hours do you take to vacuum, mop, move tables, set up for the weekly special events, and give attention to monthly items like windows or baseboards? Even if the calendar reveals the same area, program, and times, the setup could differ. This is more crucial when the janitorial work is contracted instead of completed by employees of the church. A contract crew may come after office hours and need a point of contact to help them understand the forecast for the week from a staff meeting. Special events will require advance notice so the crew or staff can be scheduled for this event. If you have several special events throughout the year, a contract crew could be utilized for special occasions to eliminate overtime for the ongoing janitorial staff. Another janitorial factor to consider is that people have also become more sensitive to the chemicals they use at home, and it is sometimes requested that people know what is utilized in the building. This will be an added cost to use greener cleaning products in the facility.

## The Kinds of Giving

"Sacred cows" that have been solicited or allowed for designated giving toward buildings or furnishings are standard in established churches. You may have attended a church where each pew had a plaque with a family name in honor or memory of someone. Sometimes a chandelier, organ, or room of the church was furnished by a family and had a plaque posted in recognition. These are all great ways to raise funds needed for more expensive furnishings or even the funds required to build a building, but they need a long-term plan for how the legacy will be honored when furnishings need to be replaced or updated. An unintended consequence of naming rights is that it cements a legacy with emotional ties. A pastoral leader should be wise when allowing or soliciting naming rights to furnishings, areas of the facility, or a building. The long-term expectations placed on the church by donors should be considered. Leaders need to understand that decisions made in the present will impact the ongoing needs and care of the congregation for the future. A master plan is one way to forecast future needs and create timelines for people to understand the present. As we age, we are reminded that all things vanish with time and nothing is forever, so we must steward what we invest our lives into as we strive to follow Christ.

Designated giving can be a challenge as people may desire to be a part of a trip, event, ministry, or project and therefore place money toward the need. The Internal Revenue Service (IRS) has guidelines on how designated giving should be collected in non-profit organizations to be considered a tax-deductible donation. Wise leaders understand these rules and have a plan that follows the guidelines when dealing with designated giving for the property. Another issue is when someone gives a gift but can only fund part of the need. Suppose others do not join in giving toward the need. In that case, money is given and designated in a fund but can only be used if a cheaper option is available or more money is given or set for that purpose. This leads to the discussion of certain ongoing designated funds that a church needs, for example, a continuous building fund. Ongoing building needs will arise and can only sometimes be covered by the general ongoing budget. A student ministry space, prayer garden, gym, or new worship center may be needed at some point or never become a reality. A master plan and a strong building fund allow these special projects or individual ideas that cannot be fully funded to have options for still benefitting the church.

## Buying and Financing Projects

As churches need to design and build a new space or redevelop and repurpose an existing space, the overall costs often result in a capital campaign to raise the necessary funds to achieve the project goal. Capital campaigns and when to build deals with many factors from the state of the economy, giving fatigue, or the capacity to pay for the project. Fundraising is not for the faint of heart. Whether you are remodeling, building a new building, or acquiring property, financing the project is only part of the battle.

The organization must invest in oversight of the project. The challenge is to cast a compelling vision that will cause people to share their excess income and savings. We will discuss more on this in the next chapter. The property encompasses the land, structures, furnishings, fixtures, and equipment. A church can become landlocked, which will cause the future expansion to be limited. The organization's parking, ministry space, and overall land needs must be considered. Each organization must do what they believe is best for them, but I recommend purchasing adjacent land as it becomes available.

Building a new facility and casting a vision is fun and exciting for both you and your people. Watching the building develop from concept to construction and completion is also a momentum boost for the church. However, the Bible speaks of someone who goes out and builds without first counting the cost.[1] Costs to the ongoing operating budget is a factor that a church should consider when counting the costs of construction. Some overlooked areas include insurance, utilities, maintenance, and janitorial operating expenses. The case could be made that those must be factored into the overall building costs.

Another aspect to consider is the leadership credibility to persuade the congregation to build and then walk in unity to do so. A leader does not want to sell the idea but lets the vision guide. The overall costs are the primary factor for one to consider. Asking questions and ensuring the leadership represents the church, ministries, and various perspectives is crucial to think holistically about what is built, how it is

---

[1] Luke 14:28.

constructed, and how pliable it will be for current and future ministry needs.

A remodeling project is like building, and the process will depend on the scale of the remodel. Existing space being remodeled is challenging, and people are sometimes not as excited about a remodel because they may not understand the why or do not want their space or seat to be changed. Some members may have never tackled remodeling projects over the years at their homes, or people may not consider that their Wal-Mart Supercenter is now gray and used to be taupe. Most chain stores have an exterior and interior remodel plan based on years of life, and carpet or other flooring types have an average lifespan. The roof, HVAC systems, kitchen equipment, and other major cost units also have life expectancies so that the organization can plan for replacement. A major remodel plan can have a primary rationale that makes sense to leaders but does not translate to the individual church member. If you establish the goal early and show the need to care and plan for property improvements, then remodeling will seem more reasonable to your people.

## Making Room for Growth

A property becomes a personal connection to the church as people experience life within the walls. A mom remembers baby dedications, her kids' baptisms, and weddings. A grandfather walks through the hallways and remembers when his parents helped construct the fellowship hall, where his kids were married, and even where family members' funerals occurred. Younger generations do not have the same kind of connection to the local church building as previous generations. Although adults have cared well for the facility, the future property strategy is shifting toward a missional focus on people rather than a real estate investment through the property. As you cast a vision for your property and programs, the challenge of raising the funds needed will require time, wisdom, and strategy. You want to avoid becoming a beggar or overselling the need to your people.

Thinking outside the box during seasons of growth has been attempted in many ways over the years. Modular office and classroom space can be moved onto the property to provide additional space. Adjusting schedules and moving people to lobbies, gathering spaces, multiples of at least three groups in a large room like a fellowship hall or gym, or utilizing church offices for adult small groups can help expand the square footage. People can be squeezed for a season, but these are not ideal group meeting spaces.

Parking, worship, and preschool are the three trigger points for considering more space. People do not like to circle the parking lot looking for a parking place. Urban environments deal with street parking challenges and public transit access. Each physical setting will have its challenges over time. A leader will help their congregation plan and maintain their property. Sometimes as leaders, you need to be patient with people and over-communicate the vision so they can come alongside and understand the need or overcome their connection to a space. Partnerships may be an option for parking or hosting a ministry or aspect of your work when space is a challenge. Schools, strip malls, or vacant parking lots can extend parking if you can bus people to campus. A church can sometimes reimagine its space by cleaning out storage areas and converting them into usable space, sharing space with offices, or even considering places for tweaks in how they are set up. Creating a balcony, bumping out some walls, trading growing ministries for larger space, and moving groups that needed less space are just a few ways of expanding existing space. The overall space plan is a chess match as a ministry grows and people move as necessary to accommodate the ministry's needs.

## Policies and Procedures

Your church should have a facility usage policy that outlines what can and cannot occur in various places within the facility and who is allowed to use the facility. We will discuss this more later. We desire to be open to the members, community, and outside organizations, but these opportunities must match the overall vision and mission of the church. For example, a school wanting to host a dance in the gym may be an opportunity, but that kind of event might not coincide with your church values. A wedding that aligns with values contrary to Scripture would not be a worship service I would schedule or lead. Each event, activity, and ministry needs to be scheduled in view of ministry alignment and business factors for cleaning the facility, setting up the space, coordinating facility usage, and liability. The business side is often not considered when a minister wants to schedule space for their event or a layperson desires to utilize the church facility. You must help people understand the time involved to clean and set up, and the facility's availability. Many may claim they will handle the set up and cleaning, but over years of ministry, this has proven to be an unreliable approach to facility management.

## Conclusion

As you approach the property of your church, first begin by being thankful that you have a facility. Many people around the world would love to have a place to have Bible study, worship services, offices, fellowship, and designated places for kids. Second, develop a plan for maintenance of the resources that has been entrusted to you from previous generations as an act of stewardship. Third, remember that you enjoy clean facilities, and the church should have the same atmosphere each week. These are three aspects that you can use to have a positive approach to your property management. You will always have the unexpected items, just like at your home. These can only be handled as they occur, and major investments with roofs or air conditioning will be needed as a building ages. Plan for maintenance and coordinate your facilities usage to align with your mission priorities, and you will be able to steward the gift that has been entrusted to your care.

## Chapter 3:

# Fiscal Development and Management

Change in your pocket is a great sound for a kid with a piggy bank. The joy of each coin dropping into the bank creates a sense of wealth. The discovery of money becomes a desire for more at a young age as the thought occurs that this newfound item could buy you things you want at a store. Family members might help you fill that piggy bank and purchase those items. Sometimes, people at church feel like pocket change or a little extra cash is enough to keep the bills paid. Many do not understand the overall costs and the scope of need for missions, ministry, operations, and maintenance. Handling money sparks many reactions and emotions. Each of us approaches the concept of income and wealth through the lens of our families, experiences, and beliefs. When you put those factors together, financial stewardship within the congregation involves diverse perspectives. Most marriage counselors cover finances in premarital counseling because two adults merging houses, budgets, and finances is often a hot topic. They spend, save, and invest differently, and now must manage finances together. Navigating finances is a personal matter that causes strife, from a child wanting money for a toy to an adult making dreams happen on a budget.

An example from the Bible of the various approaches to finances is highlighted through the lens of a widow. This story resonates with me because my father passed away when I was young, and I saw how my mother sacrificed and faithfully served the church as a widow. Her example reminds me of Luke's account of various offerings given to the temple treasurer. You can picture the flow of the crowd as they enter or exit with people of each social class dropping their offering in a designated place, much like many churches today with various offering styles due to the COVID-19 pandemic. It is hard to notice one person and what they place or do not place in the container. However, Jesus noticed and explained that the widow dropped only two small coins but gave more than everyone else.[1] This is difficult to understand as churches praise a significant gift or a pledge to a new building. I have heard it stated that what is important is not equal gifts but equal sacrifice. In an economy where people struggle to find margin in their lives whether they are lower, middle, or upper class, giving requires sacrifice as people look at their end-of-the-month bank balance. Churches should not focus on flashy amounts but the faithfulness of God's people to give gifts according to their ability. The widow's two coins are a great example that giving is unto the Lord and not others' opinions.

Finances in the organization must first be understood within biblical teaching and from the perspective of personal stewardship. Jesus mentioned money often in his teaching. In this chapter, we will address several practical financial processes outlined from a biblical foundation. Business practices for accounting and banking will then be applied through a Scripture-informed foundation. The Bible should always drive the philosophy related to working with and utilizing money in the church. One place where Jesus deals directly with money and the management of money is found in Luke 16:1–13. A manager had been dishonest and was brought before his boss and questioned by his owner. The manager was worried about losing his position, so he acted shrewdly and collected on debts by reducing the amounts owed. In verse 11, Jesus posed a question that is worthy to ponder in this chapter: "So if you have not been faithful with worldly wealth, who

---

[1] Luke 21:1–4.

will trust you with what is genuine?"[2] He then follows this question with another for a manager of finances also to consider: "And if you have not been faithful with what belongs to someone else, who will give you what is your own?"[3] The people who deal with making and managing the church's finances should first be faithful givers to the church. Jesus makes this point clear in verse 13: "No servant can serve two masters, since either he will hate one and love the other, or he will be devoted to one and despise the other. You cannot serve both God and money."[4]

## The Right Perspective

Each organization must have a bird's eye view of finances that informs budgeting processes for the overall needs of missions, ministries, personnel, and property. We like having money left over in our private accounts after paying our monthly expenses and bills, and people prefer to avoid cutting it too close or having to be creative to stretch their money to the end of the month. Any church will operate in a way that reflects the families that comprise the ministry; however, an organization must also adhere to biblical guidelines for dealing with tithes and offerings.

A non-profit religious organization has outside guidelines placed upon it because of tax laws. The financial aspects of the church also have some business organizational best practices and procedures that should be adhered to. The IRS, bank policies, and non-profit laws are outside influences on fiscal policies that have insight into an organization's process for fiscal responsibility. Introductory accounting teaches one basic equation: total assets equal the sum of liabilities plus equity. A church also needs this basic rule when dealing with the accounting of its finances. Any organization must identify and locate its assets. A church has a property that includes instruments, equipment, and furnishings. An inventory must be conducted, and values should be counted as assets. The land and buildings account for the most significant percentage of owned assets. Any unrestricted funds in the bank would count toward the asset portfolio. Liabilities include a mortgage against the property or other loans, designated funds, or the

---

[2] Luke 16:11.
[3] Luke 16:12.
[4] Luke 16:13.

organization's outstanding bills in its monthly financial report. Equity is figured once all the liabilities are deducted. If you had a mortgage on a church property for 1 million but the property was worth 3 million, your equity would be 2 million.

## The Income

The starting place for an organization's finances begins with its income. Each congregation needs to have a forecast of ministry funds each year. We all like to be on the receiving side of cash, whether for eating out, catching a movie, or paying a bill. The Bible instructs us that giving is better than receiving, and we understand that to mean financial giving. However, it is hard to have a preference for giving because we receive gifts from our earliest memories. Maybe it began with a Valentine's card, Easter basket, birthday present, report card prize, end of school year happy, or Christmas present. Many people have received these kinds of gifts throughout their lives and have difficulty grasping the concept of giving. Even in the church, when there is a surplus of funds, some can struggle when the leadership suggests giving some away to missions instead of directly spending the funds within the congregation on themselves or their facilities or ministries. One of my favorite personal application books in the Bible is James. A practical application that has helped me with giving is Jas 3:16, "for where there is envy and selfish ambition, there is disorder and every evil practice." Paul's letter to the church at Philippi contains several truths that are great reminders for us to "do nothing out of selfish ambition or conceit, but in humility consider others as more important than yourselves. Everyone should look not to his own interests, but rather to the interests of others."[5] In the church, this personal perspective informs the congregation's approach to the church budget and how it leverages income and assets for the kingdom.

As an organization, you need to consider all your income streams. The primary source of income will be tithes and offerings. You may sell items throughout the year that can be income, such as instruments, equipment, and used items to generate revenue. Fundraisers for camp or bake sales for missions is also additional income. In most denominations, special offerings focused on state, national, or international missions are passed through the organization to another entity. You

---

[5] Phil 2:3–4.

may have designated sources of income for the building, different projects or ministries, or scholarships for trips and school. Auxiliary services are another way a church could receive payment through a participation fee for an event, activity, retreat, or sport. A tuition-based program for Mother's Day Out, a weekday preschool program, or a private Christian school operated by the church are additional sources of income. You could have rental income from a house owned by the church or from the church's facilities or other rental assets. A church may have stocks, investment accounts, or savings accounts that yield interest. Each organization must consider the complete fiscal income picture to understand financial standing. The essential accounting function is that assets equal the sum of liabilities plus equity.

## *Tithing and Giving*

The standard approach to finances in most churches is that the people will give in some way to their church. Some debate has occurred over the years about tithing, what percentage a person should give, and what constitutes an offering. I understand the desire to be accurate to the biblical text as we consider percentages of income as a tithe and offerings that are in addition to a tithe. One purpose of this chapter is to explore the finances of the organization as they are collected and then distributed on behalf of the organization for its stated objectives. Many will debate over money, but the mature Christian posture should be from an attitude of generosity as good stewards since everything is from the Lord and our lives are then offered back to him through humble obedience. As leaders, it is vital that we understand our theology and positions toward finances as we lead others to be faithful in their giving to the organization. Mark Deymaz and Harry Li provide a warning in *The Coming Revolution in Church Economics:*

> As with the growing burden on America's middle class, marginal increases in religious giving, and a shift in generational approaches to giving, rapidly changing demographics—given income disparity between people groups—will greatly affect church budgets. Such things will likely lead to a loss in revenue and to a fundamental reshaping of the way congregations are funded.[6]

---

[6] Mark Deymaz and Harry Li, *The Coming Revolution in Church Economics: Why Tithes and Offerings Are No Longer Enough, and What You Can Do about It* (Grand Rapids: Baker, 2019), 39.

Many leaders and organizations are not prepared to navigate financial changes in the church. Most budgets are constructed from a historical past rather than a forecast of a changing landscape. Money is referenced throughout Scripture and still makes many cringe when the topic is mentioned at church. As a child, the term *treasure* was the recurring theme when the pastor addressed the subject of money. Jesus used this reference in his teaching during the Sermon on the Mount. He stated, "for where your treasure is, there your heart will be also."[7] This verse was cemented into me as a child as I went forward and put money in the little white church building on my birthday each year. This was a small reminder that our lives and everything we had could be offered back to the Lord. The practice has been abandoned over the years, but churches should still consider how all ages need to be instructed about treasure.

## Transparency and Terms

Fraud has caused many to lose trust in organizations if transparency with how funds are utilized is not forthcoming. Rollie Dimos recommends that organizations prevent fraud and inform employees of potential issues. The day-to-day operations includes receiving income, paying bills, recording transactions, and preparing reports, and only some employees will be involved in this process of following controls and safeguards for managing the finances. Each employee is responsible for being a good steward of the organization's resources.[8] We will now explore some best practices for churches to safeguard finances and assets in their day-to-day operations. Ministers and pastors, often feel the least prepared to lead in the church's financial operations. Regardless of size, ministers feel inadequate in dealing with the organization's finances but still have the expectations placed upon them by the church to raise funds and manage those funds in a way that honors the Lord.[9]

Basic accounting defines three terms ministry leaders must understand regarding the church's finances: assets, liabilities, and equity.

---

[7] Matt 6:21.

[8] Rollie Dimos, *Integrity at Stake: Safeguarding Your Church from Financial Fraud* (Grand Rapids: Zondervan, 2016), 13.

[9] Aubrey Malphurs and Steve Stroope, *Money Matters in Church* (Grand Rapids: Baker, 2007), 13.

Assets are the cash available to be spent, items owned, and any out-standing balances owed to the organization. The general fund checking account is an example of cash assets, and a church van or piano are items owned by the organization. Refunds for a camp or curriculum returned to the publisher are assets owed to the church. If you do not know what the church owns, an inventory of the furnishings, equipment, and other items should be conducted and maintained. Liabilities are monies owed to creditors and can include a church credit card, a contract with future obligated expenses, or a mortgage for the property. Equity is the organization's net worth, which is calculated by the total value of assets minus the total liabilities. You need to be aware of this simple equation for equity so the financial reports make sense as they are calculated.

## Budgeting Areas and Processes

Accounting processes are needed in any organization. Simple software like QuickBooks can be utilized to track financials and be able to print reports of expenses, income, or payroll. You can outsource some or all of these tasks to an accounting firm. You will also need a system that allows you to track and provide annual giving records to each family unit.

Giving records are statements of gifts to the church per calendar year and not the organization's fiscal year. These records are needed to file taxes. The burden is on the taxpayer to clarify the amount given to non-profit organizations. The IRS produces a non-profit guide each year that explains specific rules for handling tithes, offerings, and designated gifts. Gifts can be cash, stock, property, or other gifts in kind to the organization.[10]

Estate gifts are not promoted each weekend during a worship service, but as people age, churches should consider helping their people consider a last gift in their will. The Baby Boomer generation is larger than Generation X, and thus giving will go down in the coming decades with fewer tithing adults. If a church helps its people consider estate gifts, a replacement for tithing income could help sustain its work.

---

[10] "Tax Guide for Churches and Religious Organizations," https://www.irs.gov/pub/irs-pdf/p1828.pdf, 29.

Income-generating ministries and services create some accounting considerations with the IRS based on receipts, local and state sales
tax, and property tax based on the facility's square footage. An example is a coffee shop operated by the church in an area of the building
open to the public. The county may charge property tax for that part
of the facility being utilized as a coffee shop. Sales tax must be paid
based on goods sold, and employees become part of the human resource consideration for taxes and compensation. Churches can rent
their facilities in income-generating ways with weddings and outside
organizations. Your policy and procedures manual must define the difference between ministry and income generating activities to clarify
rental versus ministry partnerships.

Assets are different for each organization, but an organization's
primary assets are cash on hand, savings, buildings, and properties.
Stocks, bonds, investments, and rental property are other assets that
some churches have in their portfolios. A general fund of three months'
income is a minimum safe cash flow operating balance.

Tithes and offerings need a process for being collected and
counted. Offering plates passed during a worship service are collected
and placed into a money bag that is then processed and counted by a
team of three unrelated adults. A rotating group of counters allows no
one person to have sole access to the church's money. The financial
administrator or treasurer processes online giving through websites,
applications, and mailed-in or dropped-off donations in the office. The
plurality of options for giving has created more processes since the
offering plate is no longer the primary method of collecting of tithes
and offerings. Online giving is no longer an emerging type of giving. Many churches during the COVID-19 pandemic stopped passing
offering plates and provided stationary giving boxes placed in their
facility. Some churches were already set up for online giving.

Church credit cards and how they are allowed to be used vary by
organization. Some keep the credit card from leaving the property and
only utilize it for purchases from within the offices. Other organizations have multiple cards and place the staff members' names on the
card with the organization's name, making each person accountable
for their expenses on the card each statement cycle. Some organizations choose to have prepaid cards or the church's name listed. Some
churches have also decided not to have a credit card on behalf of the
organization.

Purchasing is another component of fiscal responsibility that requires a detailed process. Each person responsible for a cost center of the budget should follow the same process for spending funds from their area(s) of responsibility. A detailed process should outline how a ministry requests funds and then receives approval. Then the purchase can be made utilizing approved methods of payment. Most organizations have a purchase order system for the approval process and have spending levels for people within the organization that can authorize purchases.

Reimbursable accounts allow ministerial staff to spend money for education, conferences, hospitality, and mileage for business reasons and turn in receipts and expenses for reimbursement. The policy and procedures manual should outline how these funds can be utilized in submitting and being reimbursed for the expenses. If the IRS process for reimbursable accounts is not followed, this benefit becomes taxable income. For more information, download the minister tax guide from Guidestone.[11]

Fiscal areas can be problematic, and accountable processes for tracking the finances are needed. However, organizations can also struggle with money when the income misses the projected budget. As finances get tighter, people tend to stress or scrutinize ministries and expenses differently than when the budget is fully funded. Making a leaner budget work or implementing a reduced budget challenges more aspects of the church than its finances. When you need to reshape the budget on a dime, here are some considerations for review. To begin, know what you can work with to pay your expenses. Second, consider the overall financial picture. Has your organization been in this position before and simultaneously in the calendar year? If you can show how the issue was navigated before with some ways to improve that strategy, you will have greater buy-in from your leadership. Considering the past, factor in the reserves that could be jeopardized with salaries, bills, or other fixed expenses if depleted. The third step would be to consider ways to trim costs on fixed expenses with utilities, change insurance deductibles or coverages (not always wise long-term), or trim other fixed expenses through cost-saving measures. You can then look for the next layer of budget cuts and see where you can

---

[11] "Ministers' Tax Guide," *Guidestone*, https://www.guidestone.org/Updates/Ministers -Tax-Guide.

trim to save money. This can be a challenging measure mid-year when some ministries have already spent a large portion of their budget and other ministries have future budgeted events and plans. Finally, you must begin to shut down, cancel, or suspend ministries or activities until the financial stability improves.

Here are steps to reshape your budget:

1.  Know what you have to work with.
2.  Consider the holistic financial picture.
3.  Consider ways to trim costs with fixed expenses.
4.  Begin the process of eliminating ministry expenses until the finances improve if the first three steps have not helped improve the overall financial picture.

## Fraud and Audits

Fraud is an unfortunate reality in the world of personal and business finances. You may have been a victim of stolen identity or a scam. The church is another place scammers are trying to make money. As finance managers deal with invoices and outside companies, it is essential to ensure they are not misrepresenting an actual business. One example is a church that was building a new worship center, and a scammer stole a large sum acting as the construction company doing the work. Scammers are posing as the companies' people do business with and trying to collect payment for services. There are several types of scams, and your church financial team needs to be informed.[12]

Audits are different for each church because some have processes that require an internal audit as well as an external audit. Judas was a greedy disciple, as we learn from John 12. Jesus and the disciples had stopped to see Lazarus, Martha, and Mary on the journey to observe the Passover. As they are preparing a meal, Mary anoints Jesus's feet. Judas comments that the costly perfume could have been sold to feed the poor. The Scripture records that "he didn't say this because he cared about the poor but because he was a thief. He was in charge of the money-bag and would steal part of what was put in it."[13] Churches can have staff or members with access to funds that also take from the

---

[12] "Scams Targeting Small Business," https://www.incorp.com/help-center/business-articles /top-scams-targeting-small-business.

[13] John 12:6.

money-bag. Audits enable the organization to ensure funds are spent and directed as intended.

A word of caution concerning money: Some ministry leaders may be tempted to use money as a means of control or manipulation. They may worry that if the congregation is not supportive of the church's direction, giving could change and tithes could be withheld. Each of us grew up with varied social and economic lives that could differ in adulthood. Ministry leaders may feel compelled to use ministry funds to enhance their status or lifestyle by buying items for the "ministry" they cannot afford. God's economy outlined throughout the Scriptures does not reflect control of people through finances. He tells us not to rely on money but rather to be free givers regardless of our wealth.

A wise friend once shared with me that you never earn enough to arrive at a place of feeling secure because your lifestyle and relationship with money will change as you have more to work with. I have seen this happen in congregations and in families as their money situations improve and their approach to finances change. We must maintain a biblical perspective on money, whether in poverty or wealth, no matter what our current situation may be.

# Chapter 4:

# Programming Development and Management

M inistry has pivoted over the years to have various programs. You may have never heard of the Baptist Young Peoples Union, Church Training, Discipleship Training, Acteens, or Royal Ambassadors. People that do not grow up in the local church do not have the foundation of former programming or traditions that some may resonate with in the congregation. As names and programs change with time, the programming concept becomes more about practice and naming. This chapter will address aspects of the programming philosophy while addressing the management needed to coordinate everything offered into systems. Here is a question for you to ponder as we trace this process in your organization: How do you decide what is offered through your church?

The ministries and organizational affiliations listed online are one aspect of programming since people go to social media and the internet to review what is offered and understand the organization's affiliations. Another part of programming is the church calendar that organizes people and events that fill the facility on Sundays and throughout the week. Worship and Bible studies with various discipleship and age-graded opportunities occur each week as the church gathers. The church has additional missions, worship, and discipleship options with age-graded activities during their mid-week schedule. Sometimes a legacy group of fifty-five and above has events, the student ministry has a weekend outreach, and various ministry teams and committees meet during the week. Often men's and lady's groups will meet for Bible study and fellowship. The list is numerous, and this chapter cannot cover all the different events your church may choose to schedule. Throughout this chapter, different aspects will be presented to help you consider what should be factored in when programming the overall work and schedule of the church.

Planning and organizing have been required in programming an organization's overall work for generations. This concept has been transferred from the business world to the church through scientific management models developed during the twentieth century. Frederick Taylor is known as the father of scientific management as his ideas flourished in the early part of the twentieth century.[1] Several other schools of thought emerged in business in the struggle between being more efficient with time and production. Other theorists valued the team or people and personnel development more than the production. Scientific and administrative management with process and programming eventually moved into a period focused on human relations, studying the worker or the informal relations within the organization. The next phase became known as the Behavioral Science Movement, which focused on work behavior within an organization. The last focus became workers and their potential for improvement instead of a focus on the organizational improvement.[2] As you approach programming in the church, remember these movements. The focus should be to improve the disciple's ability to follow Christ and serve his church. Do not let your priority be the programming of the organization over your people.

Each aspect of the organization needs to be planned and organized to accomplish the intended purpose of each activity. Programming needs to be coordinated effectively for the organization due to the need for more oversight of an approved plan. Leaders should always start with church-wide prayer. Next, the planning should include the

---

[1]  Kenneth Coley, *The Helmsman* (Colorado Springs: ACSI, 2006), 17.
[2]  Coley, 23.

vision and mission of the church, followed by objectives and goals to execute and achieve the vision and mission. You may employ a different leadership forecast than the vision, mission, objectives, and goals. Still, the key is ensuring you have a system for how you approach your organization's plan for ministry. Books have been written on how leadership can develop programs and organizations toward executing a strategy. Refer to the two chapters that deal with finances, policies, and procedures, which rely on the planning of programming to inform areas of oversight and financial needs of the organization's planned activities.

## People and Property

People and property are two crucial components in organizing the plan toward an executable strategy. This phase is more challenging for leaders because of the differences between the organization's younger and older generations. Various age groups have different perceived ministry needs and expectations. People's attendance varies, from almost weekly to seldom. Relationships are more critical to some adults than the ministry programs that are offered. Older adults find more importance in the buildings and structure of the organization, whereas younger adults find a deeper connection to people than the structure. Mapping the organization is one of the challenges to programming since some ministry and discipleship interaction during the week is not scheduled but organic among the people. Even though the organic exists in the church, the overall events planned through the church are programmed and need coordination. Churches reflect a similar map to their organization through their leadership structure and ministry options offered each week. In the past, many congregational-led churches mirrored each other through the standards provided for organizing the church and its ministries. Diversity among ministries and the various approaches to what a church should provide have created more regional separation between churches.

Several challenges have arisen through this new diversity of entrepreneurial approaches for organizing the local church into a coherent system. If you do not like a hierarchal structure and prefer a more decentralized relational structure, then the way programs are organized and relate to one another will be different. Organizing the overall program into a system that allows for communication with the people is needed, especially in the church, where everyone is not always present at the same time. In addition, daily decisions must be executed with people, property, ministry, and finances. It's a challenge to establish a leadership structure in a system where people understand doctrinal and biblical accountability, the teachings of the church, and the leadership authority process for the organization's business. Another challenge for the church is that entrepreneurial approaches have created a lack of understanding of what occurs and thus a need for orientation meetings or clear communication plans for programs. A banner with a date, time, location, and logo will not suffice to articulate what is happening.

People have varied work experiences with structures and processes. They may have observed a pyramid strategy with a foundation that escalates to the point. Others may be familiar with a flow chart process beginning with the top leader and flowing down through each layer of the organization. Some might be more familiar with decentralization, which looks like a diamond as people make different points but come in and out to make decisions and work together. Since churches are unique in their governance, it can be a challenge for people to understand the programming processes when they are operating within a new structure. Suppose you have laypeople in your church with military backgrounds. They might expect a flow chart system and exert their influence into any process they think relates to their position with little flexibility. An entrepreneurial businessperson that has been successful will be more hesitant to execute a half-hearted plan because he or she has learned from his or her failures. People's perspectives must be factored into how your organization approaches its administrative programming.

## Leadership and Programming

Administering the work of the church centers around how programming is executed. Pastors, ministers, and directors of ministries have a great responsibility to oversee all programs at the church. This is one of the places where a pastoral ministry administration informed by a Scripture-based model may conflict with a business model. Scripture states that an overseer will give an account of their ministry and leadership. Some lay leaders in a congregational model for the local church desire to make decisions without pastoral oversight of people, property, or programs related to schedule, leadership, or finances. Their experience in the world and position on a committee empowers some lay leaders to feel more in control of the church program and set the agenda when the Lord, in his church, gave the title overseer to the pastor, not the committee chairman or deacon. Pastoral leadership is needed to develop the program system for the church's work.

Many leaders roll their eyes at the thought of this process, but it is a necessary aspect of the organization. One example of this is the administrative calendaring for facilities. Many people assume someone is coordinating the facilities and calendar and do not consider the process. The organization needs to know the time and place of each activity, whether a one-time event, scheduled weekly ministry, or a meeting. If you serve in an established church that has chosen to give out keys to lay leaders over the years, then you may have a church culture that does not value coordinating facility usage with the church office. They unlock the door and turn on the lights and HVAC trusting that all will be fine because they will make sure the facility is as they found it when they are finished. I remember a senior member explaining that the fellowship hall was her extended living room for when her family had large gatherings and that specific dates on the calendar were ongoing from year to year. She expected the ministry event on the church calendar to be canceled because her family always had the first Saturday in December. This unwritten rule created a challenge far beyond a date or calendar issue. Some church members have this mindset about programs and do not understand the need to prioritize the primary aspects, such as ministry programs and events, before other elements are placed onto a calendar. People can sometimes be consumed with their own needs and are not concerned that their interests are conflicting with the overall program needs of the church.

This can also happen among ministry leaders as they value their ministry more than others. Turf wars are an expression one might expect outside of the church, but turf wars can be exposed when trying to program the work within the church. This bias can be exposed when an entitled ministry leader forgets to schedule an annual event and another ministry schedules that date. Conflicts with programming between leaders or ministries are unfortunate because each person needs to be ministered to, have fellowship opportunities, and feel a connection to the local church. Managing the programming needs of each ministry through processes and systems that ministry leaders and volunteers understand limits confusion and deescalates potential turf wars.

# The Importance of Systems

Organizational management allows the church to clarify who is responsible for everything it decides to include in its programmed activities, ministries, events, and properties. A program's priority needs to be established and communicated to the congregation so everyone knows the philosophy that drives the programming. Planning the scope of work so that a system can be created to place volunteers, assign space, and allocate all the additional resources needed is an administrative process that, for many people, is undervalued in the church. People see the platform and those on stage or in critical positions but never see the countless hours of work behind the scenes. A meeting with representatives from all the ministry areas can be helpful in this process. A church council or ministry leadership team approach can help bring staff and critical volunteers together to discuss and coordinate the church's ministries.

Systems for programming can help arrange people, ministries, and facilities into a scheduled process that is clear and understandable by the organization's leadership. Utilizing a software system designed for ministries like Church Community Builder or Realm will help you organize your members, prospects, and finances. These systems can also be utilized to track your ministries' activities and details: "Planning Center is a set of software tools to help you organize information, coordinate events, communicate with your team, and connect with your congregation."[3] A software system that allows you to communicate, coordinate, and connect is needed as your church grows in people and ministry.

Ministries can become programming nightmares when people try to do them their way. A kind senior adult man once shared how the church should seek his approval before making any plans because he was the gatekeeper of all programming. He may not have used those exact words, but he was communicating he was in charge and the keeper of the unwritten policies the staff and ministry leaders were expected to follow. A smaller established church may have its version of Robert's *Rules of Order* in the flesh, as this kind gentlemen functioned in "his" church. Developing transparent processes for coordinating and scheduling the church's programs can aid in addressing controlling people. Ministry effectiveness can also increase as a system is put in

---

[3] Planning Center, https://www.planningcenter.com.

place that considers the people and their needs and the coordination of schedule and time that allows more people to be involved.

When developing your processes and systems for coordinating the church's programs, people should be the first consideration. However, the organization must also factor the property needs into the process. Each event requires setup, cleaning, and resources that must be planned in advance. The support staff needs to be on the schedule. Items may need to be ordered, an event may conflict with another in the same scheduled space, or the number of programs may overburden the team and overwhelm the system, inhibiting the execution of quality events. Many ministers or lay leaders do not factor in organization support needs for programming HVAC or the complications of multiple groups sharing spaces with different setup needs. A programming system helps the office monitor when another group requests to utilize the church and what is available when requests are made.

A ministry can be a part of your programmed activity and not occur on your property or within your facility. Notice the distinction between property and the facility. You may have a playground, rec field, or pavilion that people utilize for family events or a ministry function. People also use their property or residence to host an event, Bible study, fellowship, or overnight retreat. If the church programs the event through the church-established process, the organization's umbrella policy should be considered regarding whether it extends to an outside location. Churches need to consider the ministry impact of events and how to utilize property whether owned, borrowed, or rented. Still, organizational factors must be remembered as events are scheduled through the organization's established policies.

### Questions to Consider

When it comes to programming, organizations have some questions that they should consider. For example, Why does the church employ its ministries through programming? This is vital because people need to understand the plan. If something does not go according to plan, people will ask who approved it and why it was allowed. Anything that is programmed will need a rationale as to why it was on the property and why the people involved were approved as leaders of the organization. This issue then focuses on who was in charge, and if they knew what was happening. Did they know the safety protocols, have enough chaperones, or understand the facility enough to know the risks? These questions are not fun but become critical if something happens on a property during a programmed event, a side note reminder that troubles always occur. The church can only manage and reduce the risk associated with programming, not eliminate it.

Ponder another question: How do we arrange a process for programming people and property to ensure that the vision and mission of the church are accomplished? Everything that is planned must be organized to ensure that the primary elements of the church have priority when it comes to timing, marketing, communication, facilities, and finances. The church does not desire to be a people that has overcommitted its bandwidth to the point that the primary functions are diminished. The congregation can weaken due to programming mismanagement or program fatigue. You may have served in a church that chronically overscheduled. The organization never intended to have program fatigue, but over the years, ministries were added with little being removed from the schedule. The organizational structure of committees, teams, and weekly ministry obligations led to mismanaged people and properties overwhelmed with all that was expected of them.

Consider this scenario: A church has a hierarchical decision-making structure with a decentralized ministry alignment for people and ministries to relate to one another. In this hybrid structure attempting to unite the generations, they work hard to staff each ministry. The children's ministry requires small group and worship care for Sundays, midweek ministries, and other events as scheduled. The student ministry is staffed on Sunday mornings and Wednesday evenings, as well as for special events. Adults have small group leaders on Sundays, midweek Bible studies, and seasonal options. The worship ministry covers first impressions, choir, praise team, and media. Recreation offers different sports seasons for children that require coaches, referees, and other volunteers. Bereavement, outreach, benevolence, family ministry, discipleship, and student ministry have advisory teams for oversight of each area. Then the church has administrative committees for finance, property, and personnel. Men and women also have seasonal ministries and opportunities throughout the year. The pastor senses the tension between the overcommitted volunteers and leadership gaps as workers are unavailable for various reasons. How do you unravel this tangled web of great people and ministry while the organization is overwhelmed through its stressed programming?

Even with limited resources, each opportunity that presents itself might not need to be adopted by your organization. The congregation's personal experiences will have numerous stories of the challenges with programming in that context. These may not be transferable to another setting because each community and region has unique challenges. The problematic people or the ministries that worked incredibly well may be transferable from one location to another but do not assume the obstacles from one setting will mirror another. Programming must contextualize to understand the community calendar, school system rhythm, and the people's needs.

Leaders should avoid discouragement from people who think the process does not apply to them or do not see how challenging it is to lead people to work together as a team. Sometimes people resist each idea or program as a default due to a negative experience. As a leader, continue to love them and cast a compelling vision to join you on the journey. These challenges often find themselves in an organizational environment that could support them over time as the programming process is realized.

Consider the unintended indication that occurs through programming. When an event will occur can indicate a priority that is unintended. Due to the day and time, it is the most valued part of the program for the people. You may have observed this based on where a small group meets or when ladies' Bible study is scheduled. This can be unintentional, but people perceive it differently. Property aspects can have unintended communication as well. When a process for planning and organizing the church's work is not in place, the assignment of time or a room location on the property can communicate that it is of the utmost importance to the church. Unfortunately, some men have sought the office of deacon because the prominence of the communication and schedule of where and when the meetings occurred did not indicate an office of serving but of power or control. Deacons and lay leaders should be servants who can put aside their desires or their families for the good of the ministry.

Could you imagine a hospital that did not have a person coordinating room assignments or operating rooms? How hectic that would be for the staff, patients, and visitors. I cannot imagine the wait time for an x-ray, imaging, or ambulatory services if a program coordinator or service coordinator did not cover those details. You may have ended up with a three-hour wait for your appointment at a doctor's office with poor scheduling. Ministry is more efficient when you strive to have efficient systems so you can be more engaged with people.

## Conclusion

The focus of ministry should be on the people and not programs. Programming is the administrative support that prevents ministry to people from becoming entangled in scheduling and coordinating issues. Programming should be a supporting process to enhance the work with people and not take away from that work.

Ministry leaders can cause programming chaos when they do not work together as a team. A minister of music may randomly add extra rehearsals in preparation for a special program, or a volunteer ministry coordinator could decide to move their ministry meetings to a different time and day of the week without telling anyone in the church office. These types of challenges can be created when it is unclear how programming is executed or what process is non-negotiable. The pastor must help the people know who can make the decisions with programming and how the organizational structure functions. If something does not go as planned or a problem occurs, people will ask who is responsible. People need to know who they can turn to if a question needs to be answered or clarification is needed. Remember, ministry leaders, "A gentle answer turns away anger, but a harsh word stirs up wrath."[4] The process of programming is intended to strengthen the ministry of the church.

---

[4] Prov 15:1.

**Chapter 5:**

# Process Development and Management

M eet Larry, a new pastor to his congregation, who is planning for the first year. He does not know who makes decisions about different areas of the church. The backdrop of the church limits him during the interview and search committee process. In his first 90 days, the process of working with people, managing property, and developing programming is vague and open to interpretation. However, there is a man in the church who is the unofficial decision maker. Ron has served his church faithfully, but after twenty years the processes are organic and not written. One must be on the inside to know how things operate. If you work with Ron, it all goes well, but if you do not consult him first, frustrations will arise. Unfortunately, he is the keeper of the keys.

Each church has its own processes developed over time as a response to routine or a reaction to frustrations or problems. Each leader has their way of approaching work and people. Processes should work for the whole church and not just for the personalities of those developing or leading the organization. They should be incorporated to help the organization function and not be at the whim of powerbrokers in the church. Processes exist in any organization in formally established systems or informal means that communicate tradition or control. This chapter discusses strategies for different aspects of an organization, such as options for dealing with governing documents, structures for leading, and reasons for having processes to guide the people of the organization and its members in making wise choices. When the procedures are developed in understandable ways, they provide for the property, guide the funding mechanisms, and allow the programs to be ministry focused. The levers that are triggered operate as intended. As systems are needed for these processes to work within the church, leadership begins to see what policies and procedures need to be developed to allow for more detailed processes. An example is a process for working with minors in the church. This process should be developed with established systems for dealing with minors at church in preschool, children ministries, and ministries to teenagers. Policies and procedures that are age and ministry appropriate should be established that provide more structure to systems of each ministry. Even a lack of process is considered a default approach, whether the organization operates a healthy system or not.

## Developing Organizational Documents

First, let us examine developing documents that guide the church. In this chapter, we will look at specific areas where policies and procedures should be developed; however, the list will be limited due to the ever-changing landscape of ministry and society. The goal is to provide you with information to review, reconsider, and revise your policies as needed.

You may have a church constitution that explains how your organization was founded, where it exists, the purpose for its existence, the doctrinal framework of the church, and a church covenant for the members. Many churches also have a membership process and bylaws that explain how the church operates within a doctrinal framework. In addition, the bylaws may outline the agents and officers who make the legal decisions and provide leadership within the framework that is adopted. This document should explain how officers, agents, and staff are selected, the terms of service, the qualifications to serve in this capacity, the process for election, and a process for removal. An explanation of ministerial staff, ministries, and committees should be discussed in simple and direct sections, with the full details contained in a policy and procedures manual. Business matters such as conducting meetings, what constitutes a quorum, and the frequency of meetings should be explained. These areas should be limited because the policy and procedures manual should execute the governance outlined in the bylaws. Guidelines for order to govern meetings should be established. A process for conflict resolution and discipline should be considered for officers, staff, and members. The bylaws can be brief and cover the organization's various aspects and processes with the understanding that policy and procedures will guide the daily operations for staff, ministry, and members. The people, property, programming, finances, and the church office are the main areas to address within these documents.

## People

Each person within the organization should understand the process for membership at the church. In addition, the criteria and processes to serve in ministries should be written into policy and procedures for each area of the church. Moral conduct policies for staff and volunteers should also be outlined. The discussions on human resource considerations in chapter one of this book can serve as a reference as you develop policies and procedures.

## Property

Each building has unique challenges that need processes for opening and closing for special events, weekly programs, or day-to-day operations. Significant aspects of dealing with the property that a homeowner would know, like how to deal with management issues of turning off the electricity or where significant systems like HVAC or water can be found, are not always known by leaders in the church.

## Programming

Each ministry will have its processes. Preschool differs from senior adults, but some will overlap with people, property, or finances. Programming involves everything that is calendared and will need a strategy for what is required and how it will occur within the organization's structure.

## Finances

Each person overseeing a cost center needs written guidelines of expectations of fiduciary responsibility for each area they manage. Finance policies and procedures help everyone avoid mismanagement, fraud, or questionable ethics with money.

## Church Office

In recent years the process by which we approach the work in the church has pivoted to digital and less labor is needed in several areas of the church office. We have new approaches to information. Instead of printed material like the newsletter, we have digital connections through several free apps and services. Some choose to pay for services that have enhanced features for sharing information and connecting with those within the organization. Ministerial staff members have moved from passing on work to others to managing much of the work themselves since they do not need copies printed, fliers distributed, items folded or mailed, or even someone to manage their appointments and schedule. As a result, the job description of a ministry assistant and hours worked per minister have changed drastically. People have computers, tablets, and smartphones, allowing them to do more administrative work.

The pivot to the new norms brings the question of how a church should staff its office. The number of administrative assistants needed can be fewer because of changing workflow demands. This does not mean we should eliminate or diminish their work but expand their job toward more ministerial responsibilities rather than being limited to office administrative details. When your focus is on retaining the right people on your team, the assistants usually know the people within the church, vendors, ministries, and business details and have years of knowledge of the church. The gossip and gripes of people they usually deal with are common. This role can be retooled to be a ministry focus instead of office support based.

# Understanding the Needs of the Work

People do not want to put effort into something that does not move the organization toward achieving its mission. Due to changing conditions, the church will have to pivot as the workplace has in the business world. The church office is a tool to support the overall work to achieve the mission. One challenge is that schedules have become more fluid which means the church office does not have as much people traffic during the day. Here are some ideas to consider for your families and the plans of people within the church. First, what are the hours that most people would need access to people in the office? Have you tracked a month of traffic to know the peak hours and hours required for the office to be staffed? Second, should some staff work later and keep the office open on one or more days a week for those that work regular office hours to access resources, visit the office, or handle a business matter? Finally, should the office be open Wednesday evenings for midweek programming so as people are on the property, they can access support staff as needed?

This conversation leads a congregation toward seeking to understand the generational and cultural impact expected of the church office. In the current and future reality, younger generations will depend less on a physical office because they interact more in digital spaces. They handle insurance, utilities, and medical through digital outlets. As pastors have desired to be in the community, their studies have moved to coffee shops for more potential interactions. Some have found a home office to be more productive than the church office. People have desired to flex the ministerial hours with remote or home office time in their week to achieve time to devote to study and preparation. Some church members still desire to drop by or visit with their ministers as their schedule permits, so the new models impact relationship-building with the retired or people with fewer time restrictions. The flip side to the church office is that a prescribed office designation provides some layers of accountability not for hours worked as much as effort placed in the work. In an office, cross-training can occur, collaboration with team members is natural, and the ability to be available is more likely. Administrative assistants over the years have been some of the first to defend the work ethic, hours worked, or sacrifices made by the ministerial staff.

## Factors That Shape Church Office Availability: Culture, Location, and Church Size

Each community has experienced shifts in population and industry over its existence. The community could have grown or declined. Industry changes in the workforce that have impacted the community employment opportunities also affect the church office. As unemployment rises, the requests for benevolence at the office increase. If the local economy slows, the church finances usually decrease as well. Every ten years, a national event will cause a shift in most communities, the latest not being war or terror but the COVID-19 pandemic. As this virus moved across the globe, each community decided to wear masks or refuse, and you probably had people in the church with varied opinions on the issue. We also saw churches and businesses decide how they would function in light of the challenges sickness brought to the community and the people. Many people discovered new ways to approach their profession, and many businesses pivoted to new techniques to accomplish their mission and move forward. Churches were resilient through this season and provided solace for people within the church and the broader community.

The cultural impact is more involved than a pandemic or global crisis. A hot topic in national media deals with gender identity and how to navigate the gender fluidity landscape in society as a church. The gender issue deals with the same concerns with people, property, and programs but in a different way than a pandemic causes the church to adapt. In some regions assigning bathrooms by gender is an issue. This becomes a local church issue to decide if a bathroom becomes unisex or stays by gender in the church facilities. Do the programs have clearly defined guidelines regarding gender, whether a ladies' Bible study or a children's small group? The church office is the place that must field these types of questions and is the front line to helping explain these things to the outside world.

These issues are just a snapshot of the administrative challenges we face in the church and the church office culture. Cultural issues challenge the weekly routine of the church office. The pandemic challenged ministers to reconsider physical presence and time spent at the church office. Digital culture has challenged churches in communication, connectivity, and community. Churches have historically relied on being able to have informal conversations in hallways between leaders of ministries. Should the church still have print advertisements and sign-ups so people receive something they can review, remember, and respond to? The church bulletin is a prime example of something the COVID-19 pandemic caused many churches to eliminate due to moving services online for several weeks. Churches saved resources and shifted to digital communication instead. People pivoted to digital communication naturally. Many turned to online giving and no longer relied on an offering plate to be passed. The need for someone to answer the phone or stop by the office was also limited for many offices for months. These are the types of administrative questions leaders should ask while stewarding people, property, and programs. The office exists to serve the people, manage its facilities, and support the programs.

## The Essence of a Church Office

The church office supports the people by providing a place of support for families and their service in the church. Adults can use the church office for the business side of ministry, like ordering supplies, finding information, and submitting documents. Many volunteers rely on someone in an office to do this for their area of service. Some aspects such as counseling, setting up a ministry space, or packing ministry bags for the community require coordination from the office, oversight that tasks are completed as assigned, and access to the property at various times. Adult volunteers have varied availability, which creates a need to examine when the office is needed to be available for people and deliveries.

The church office supports the property by providing a structure to organize facility usage, coordinate deliveries and vendors, liaise with people and outside organizations, and maintain communication between ministries and staff.

The church office supports the programs and ministries of the church. The need for a staffed physical office has changed due to digital resources, digital curriculum, and the ability to offer many goods and services remotely and digitally.

## Staffing the Church Office

Every church, based on its size and needs, will staff the office differently but must consider the relationship of the church office with the people, property, and programs. This will allow you to develop church office policies and procedures that guide your decisions regarding your staff and volunteers. Often the church will not consider all the ways the church office could be staffed with volunteers. For instance, a receptionist position could be filled with volunteers who take a morning or afternoon shift. Another option is working with a local high school in job-related service to expand your team with support at a cheaper rate per hour or growing your team through an intern program. When positions become vacant, we often rush to fill the vacancy without consideration to reimagine the role or explore new ways to enhance the overall work.

You may think that is too risky or will reduce the office's professionalism. Remember, you are not a bank or insurance office. The church office can be ministry-focused before professionally driven standards are set. Suppose the desire is to serve the people and support the overall ministry. In that case, we must focus our efforts first on developing the people who view ministry as priority over professional standards. Personnel are in place for ministry and to support the overall work of the church. Ministers need flexibility to be away from the office to interact with people, leaders, and church members as part of their week. A pastor may need to allow the members of the ministerial team similar flexibility as they also have pastoral care responsibilities. The church staff's interactions with people should be transformational rather than transactional.

## Managing the Various Processes for a Church Office

The church office has many challenges as different generations approach their working hours differently and their work-life balance from different mindsets. As members of a congregation have different schedules, their need for an office has changed. The desire of some ministers to work off-site and be in the community has changed the concept of work-life balance in a job with duties outside of normal office hours. The challenge for administrative support staff is that they need hours that are prescribed to be available for deliveries, services, and subcontractors to perform their tasks. The balance of figuring out the church office when most pastors have been granted flexibility creates challenges. Each church must establish its hours with a rationale for the hours chosen. The Equal Employment Opportunity Commission enforces federal laws for employees in areas of discrimination and most of their oversight is for places with more than fifteen employees.[1] Churches must consider legal parameters appropriate for their local, state, and federal designations. Accountability is necessary for any size staff or church to protect the team and the church. Office

---

[1] U.S. Equal Employment Opportunity Commission, http://www.eeoc.gov.

space should be secure, and files must be stored in safe places. Everyone should not have a key to offices and legal documents in the church.

One chapter cannot adequately address every aspect a church must consider in its organizational processes with people, property, programs, and finances. Reactions to unexpected circumstances leads to the development of most church policies and procedure manuals. This is not as negative as it appears because, as Christians, we are called to believe in the best of people. However, a litigious society informs us this is not the wisest approach to these important areas. When we begin to develop a process that becomes policies and procedures, it leads to best practices for the organization. If these are not reviewed, prayed over, and revised consistently, they become obsolete quickly. People inside and outside the church are not all following Jesus, and sometimes good people can be utilized by the enemy to harm the church. So, we develop processes, policies, and procedures for prevention and responding to issues if they arise within the church. You may have the experience to accompany each aspect that has been mentioned in this chapter, but if not, consider researching the Church Tax and Law website for instructions in this critical area of your organization.[2]

Philosophy toward policy is diverse due to experience, ministry expectations, and historical factors from the church. Pastors bring their experiences and expectations to the development and interpretation of policy. A simple recommendation is to never establish a policy that you are not willing to train, assess, and maintain. You do not want to create an organizational culture that does not ethically follow the established policies of the church. A church should not set a policy to become a legalistic people but to shepherd its people, properties, finances, and programs so that it can protect those within the care of the congregation known as a flock. Tony Morgan outlines "a healthy system as a simple, replicable process to help people move from where they are to where God wants them to be."[3] He makes the point that we need systems or processes that help us because they should not just exist in one person's brain. It is common in smaller settings to hear people say, "Just see so and so, and they will get you squared away." Tony's response to this organic process is that every time someone desires to serve, a default system should be clear and readily available. One

---

[2] "Church Law and Tax," *Christianity Today*, last modified 2023, https://www.churchlawandtax.com.

[3] Tony Morgan, *The Unstuck Church* (Nashville: Thomas Nelson, 2017), 73.

person may know the process, but problems arise if the process was not put into a document, entrusted to a team, or is not scalable as the church grows.[4] A church can grow and reach more people if its processes are scalable, enabling more disciples to be equipped to serve. The challenge for many churches is that the low desire for processes or their unwillingness to create them is due to the need to control the organization and not expand or grow. A pastor cares for his flock and wants them to grow as disciples of Christ, and from this perspective, policies should be written so that reaching and making disciples is not hindered. Some people try to overprocess the organization and create policies that, unfortunately, prohibit ministry rather than allowing the freedom to execute the functions of the church well. Processes will vary by church but can help prescribe answers to recurring aspects of ministry that help people stay focused on the mission.

---

[4] Morgan, 73.

# PART 2:

# ORGANIZATIONAL CHALLENGES

A section that has the word "challenges" in the title may cause you to want to read it first because of what you are experiencing in your organization, or it may cause you to consider just skimming the topics. Paul's letters sometimes included references to challenges the congregation was facing or within their cultural community. This section will take a similar approach, as local congregations are dealing with challenges and need reassurance that they are not alone. The Lord has guided the church through generation after generation. All the answers will not be evident in these few chapters, but we will address some aspects that could provide insight into managing your organization through challenges.

Constantly connecting to others through texting, social media, and technology has brought challenges. People have instant access to real-time events and information that is only sometimes the best raw data or narrative needed. When a conflict arises, the full scope of the situation is necessary rather than just the facts, and people often make conclusions without an informed perspective.

Time is one aspect that has become more challenging to manage. Seven-ring binders are no longer the preferred scheduling method. Generational differences are the most diverse in recent memory as we have members from the "Builders" to the "Alpha" generations, a total of six possible generations. Learning to navigate the almost 100 years represented can challenge every area of ministry as people come with varied mindsets and needs each week. As you consider your ministry, you know the human challenges in your organization. The adult mindset regarding managing time, work approach, risk factors, attendance, or connection with the local church is diverse. Some older adults remember when the road in front of their house was paved for the first time, when electricity first came to their home, or even when a landline phone arrived on their street. These modern conveniences are complex for some younger adults to comprehend when they have a smartphone in their hand and consider a tough day to be when the air conditioning is not cold enough.

Diversity must be understood and addressed to overcome the organizational challenges to encourage unity in ministry. The hope of this book is that you consider your approach to people of all ages and better comprehend their perspectives. You can teach others about various approaches to teamwork and stewardship in a way that honors the Lord and effectively accomplishes the ministry. A few points in these chapters can encourage great training opportunities and discussions with your church. Take time to discuss approaches to these challenges so they are not a point of contention but a united path forward. Your organization's health depends on how challenges are confronted, navigated, and overcome so people can be strengthened and the congregation can flourish.

## Chapter 6:

# Time Management

The goal of time management or time stewardship is to increase production. The skill set helps a person perform high level tasks efficiently. The Christian has a different focus on their efficiency with time. Paul reminded the church in Ephesus, "Pay careful attention, then, to how you walk—not as unwise people but as wise—making the most of the time, because the days are evil."[1] He taught them to be lights in the world. As people of the church today, the perspective for time should be how to steward and redeem the minutes, hours, days, weeks, months, and years the Lord gives us as we live for Him.

Imagine a beautiful blue sky without a cloud in sight on a Saturday when you have no obligations or plans. People often lament a lack of margin or a rare day with nothing scheduled. The thought of an unhurried block of time is an existence that is only dreamed of by many. As we consider overcoming the challenges of managing time, we should view time as stewardship more than management. Children in the church are taught the reasons for being good stewards of money through giving of tithes and offerings. Time stewardship is an equally important lesson for growing in relationship with God, sharing the

---

[1] Eph 5:15–16.

Gospel with others, and investing talents and gifts toward kingdom impact. If church members were equipped with healthy time steward-ship, some organizational challenges would be diminished.

Many books have been written to address productivity and manag-ing, investing, or wasting time. In *How to Get Unstuck*, Matt Perman provides a concise overview of time management: "Personal effective-ness is the skill of leading yourself every day to get the right things done in the right way, for the right reason, and in the shortest possible amount of time."[2] Math is not a favorite subject for many students, but for us to ponder the topic of time stewardship, imagine fifty years of an adult's life attending and serving through the local church. Each Sunday, when the church gathers, the amount of time invested among people is a small portion of the entire week. However, each week the various ministries and opportunities amount to countless hours when combined. Multiply the time investment of showing up weekly to wor-ship and then serving through church ministries over fifty years of adulthood. The average faithful adult would then have a portfolio of worship and service in the local church for fifty years that reflects the following:

Fifty years of adulthood times fifty-two weeks per year multiplied by ten hours per week.

Allow six weeks of missing out for work, vacation, or sickness, and the total comes to 23,000 hours. What an investment of time into the local church from just ten hours per week worshipping, study-ing, teaching, serving, leading, discipling, and connecting with others. How much time do you think an adult has to steward over fifty years? The answer is a shocking 436,800 hours of stewarding their time for Christ, while balancing time with career and family.

In fifty years, a person has invested 436,800 hours of his or her life in different ways. Less than 23,000 hours on average are invested through the local church, which is about five percent of one's adult working life. Consider the percentage of energy, recreational time, or even overtime at work compared to the time spent at church or in personal spiritual habits. People sometimes have adverse reactions to the ten hours a week needed to staff church programs, but the sacrifice is not as great as some may think. Time spent is an important consid-eration for serving. But in the scope of time possibly granted to each

---

[2] Matt Perman, *How to Get Unstuck* (Grand Rapids: Zondervan, 2018), 55.

of us, it is less of a commitment to serve in church than to tithe at ten percent.

Whether people serve as full-time staff or volunteers, they are to tithe time beyond normal working hours. Time and treasure allow us to have accountability with each other. Time stewardship is often not discussed because people are at church each week, even though not always the same people. The average adult internet user spent two and a half hours per day on social media in 2022,[3] which equals seventeen and a half hours per week. Younger generations of adults will spend at least 45,500 hours on social media. If six weeks for sickness or vacation are deducted, the average adult will spend 40,250 on social media and maybe 23,000 hours serving and worshipping God over a fifty-year period. Time stewardship is a significant challenge for local congregations as people deal with more distractions.

Social changes in the COVID-19 pandemic introduced new lifestyle rhythms for work, family, church, and recreation for a season. For most people, work and school resumed in-person eventually, and church returned to regular programming. As church members returned to on-the-go rhythm with work, school, extracurricular activities, and church, they began to reevaluate their time. Some realized volunteering was less life-giving than they thought. People get worn down and give their time to essential areas of life.

Volunteer involvement and decreased attendance is a reality in the post-pandemic world. Leaders must consider how the culture of serving is decreasing among current adult volunteers.[4] An organizational map of ministries and people should also consider time as a factor, specifically expectations on adult volunteers for hours and number of events required. People and programs can be utilized to leverage each volunteer's time and make the most significant impact.

Considering the entire team and not just the minister is vital. Ministry leaders can greatly increase their effectiveness by even an hour through delegation to one person. The impact becomes exponential with a team of people of any size. Team management

---

[3] "How Much Time do People Spend on Social Media in 2023 (New Data)," *Earthweb*, last modified July 20, 2023, https://www.earthweb.com/how-much-time-do-people-spend-on-social-media.

[4] Kate Shellnut, "Church Leaders are Still Waiting for Volunteers to Come Back," *Christianity Today*, January 14, 2022, https://www.christianitytoday.com/news/2022/january/church-ministry-volunteer-gallup-survey-lifeway-wr.html.

involves stewarding the time of volunteers and paid staff so that ministry investment is not limited but multiplied. This does not diminish or eliminate the need for personal time management. The primary purpose in administration is people, and therefore stewarding people's time in the church requires a plan that leverages that resource toward kingdom impact. When we do not consider the program and overall ministry impact and recreate last year's calendar of ministry and events, we fail to consider what God has planned for the people he has brought to the ministry. We can lessen the impact if we are not intentional in what is planned and executed by the people each week.

The reality is that less than 5 percent of the average adult's time will be spent within the local church, but almost 10 percent could be spent on social media. As leaders, we cannot allow that time not to be intentionally managed for the highest impact possible. As the world continues to take and waste people's time, the church needs to gain back some of that time with community. Administrative management of people and programming will significantly impact time spent in the church. Imagine the impact of leveraging an average of eleven hours per week in ministry and service to the Lord. An increase of one hour per week would be another 2,300 hours spent in ministry, discipleship, worship, and community through the local church. If one were adventurous and invested fifteen hours, it would result in over 11,500 hours invested in fifty years through the local church.

## Ministry Time Stewardship

Training people used to be prescribed in a correspondence workbook for each program. Leaders should invest in their team to help them perform more efficiently and be more productive. The struggle for time investment is whether to train for ministry assignments or become a more mature disciple and not just an effective ministry volunteer. Each organization must consider time as a resource that needs to be stewarded as much as financial giving. The question then becomes what level of time commitment is good stewardship, and the answer will not be the same for each church, ministry, or person.

People have access to more content than ever, which allows ministry leaders to direct the influences of the people toward quality content and resources. Podcasts, apps, and online ministry tools help equip people in their areas of responsibility and help them become more engaged in the ministry. Cultivate resources specifically for the people you lead who need personal investment before you focus on a position they occupy.

Technology has created more opportunities to control the time stewardship of ministry leadership. Video-driven training can be done as a person's schedule allows instead of attending trainings at a specific time and place. Digital meetings can help ministry leaders and volunteers grow in their personal lives, work, and ministry. The church could be the place for teaching people to manage their work through time stewardship even though the secular world has been better at offering training for time management, productivity, and workflow.

Church leaders should consider time stewardship in planning and organizing people and programs. I have begun to utilize this mindset and change my terminology because it means more to me than management. The terms communicate a spiritual component to time that can easily be dismissed or neglected. Over the years, it was easy for me to prioritize financial management so that I could have more resources to do what I wanted. In my twenties, the Lord utilized a friend to teach me that the Lord owned everything, and I should steward my finances by considering my expenses, purchases, and debts through financial stewardship. Likewise, we utilize our gifts and talents in the church, which means we must be faithful in our attendance and offer our time to the ministry. We should also not expect our people to waste their time and sit through training that does not impact their lives or ministry. We must offer quality training events with relevant content and encouragement.

An organization should provide a few practical aspects for its members. First, people need resources and supplies for their assigned ministry responsibility. If they will not be provided or a supply room is not readily available, this needs to be communicated. Second, the space needs to be set up according to the offered requests for ministry needs. Volunteers may need more time to arrive early enough to search across the property for supplies and rearrange the space as needed. Third, volunteers and paid staff need to know deadlines for supply and set-up requests to be made through the church office. This will save some frustrations, texts, emails, calls, and conversations due to assumptions about space, people, or resources. Fourth, substitute leaders need the same information provided to ongoing staff and volunteers. We are responsible for administering the work so people (whom we need to accomplish the work) have leaders that steward time in the most effective way possible. In chapter eight, we will focus on workflow solutions that help people consider ways to enhance their work and preparation in a more gospel-productive manner.

## Office Time Management

Over the years, people have come by the church asking for the office team to help them with personal matters. The church staff must decide what level of allowing church members to conduct personal business is productive for the church. Relationships matter in the office but getting the entire church to give, vote, and agree upon a vision is also important. Each person has the same number of minutes, and these minutes get spent intentionally or not. The office can exist to serve personal needs, but if this is part of the objective, then it needs to be clearly stated. Administrative needs have changed over the past several years as technology allows more people to handle more on their own. For example, cell phones may be more readily used than office phones. I was recently at a church with fifteen staff members who did not have a phone system for the interoffice, just a line to the receptionist. The ministers and support staff often were somewhere else in the building, so using cell phones was a better option. The church office supports the church's work as its primary responsibility. This is a subtle distinction, but stewardship should be considered in managing the office and the staff's time.

## Personal Time Management

Work, family, friends, and unexpected events interrupt the schedule each week for various reasons. This chapter is not intended for you to feel defeated by how your time is spent. Stewardship is a lifelong process of continuing to tweak the balance of our resources to leverage more for the kingdom. I am thankful over the years to see senior adults giving their retirement for ministry. During times of disaster, the chainsaw crew or feeding unit has been staffed primarily by retired senior adults. You may have experienced attending a retreat center to find staff volunteers at the camp who were retired senior adults. Each season of our lives presents various ways for each of us to evaluate our time. People have taken a vacation as chaperones for camp, mission trips, or church events. Adults regularly give of themselves for backyard Bible clubs or Vacation Bible School during the summer.

Imagine the church today if people began to harness more time to serve through the church and its ministries. Most people struggle to trim their expenses, but time can be found for fifteen minutes, thirty minutes, or an hour. Have you ever been injured, and the doctor prescribed physical therapy twice a week for twelve weeks? As a result, schedules were adjusted, and miraculously the time to drive and participate in PT resulted in improved mobility. You survived the three-month time adjustment in ninety-minute segments twice a week. We can find time to become better stewards in our ministry if we consider how to leverage this resource of time for the kingdom.

Financial stewardship causes us to look at our budget. Calendars are important for time stewardship just as budgets are for financial stewardship. You may have a wall calendar hanging in your pantry; a Google calendar shared with family, office, and ministry; a calendar app; or a small written calendar. Either way, you keep up with important events, appointments, and people through your calendar. You may keep up with everything yourself or depend on someone else to remind you of your schedule. You may have worked with a boss that relied on an assistant or have a friend whose spouse keeps him or her on schedule. You probably also know someone content to be forgetful or late. We all serve in ministry with people that approach their calendar and time differently. This work of stewardship is to not make each person like us.

The disciples were very diverse, even in their interactions with Jesus—Thomas was a doubter, Peter liked to ask questions, and Judas worried about finances. One of the disciples was a little more anxious than the rest to move on to the next ministry stop on the tour with Jesus. One could imagine some disciples keeping track of time during long prayers. I bet during the sharing times, one of the disciples cleared his throat more than the others. I am joking, but we have all been in a church setting where someone in the group was anxious for the time to end or move on to the next thing. I like a well-run meeting that follows an agenda, and as an administrator, I am aware when people think I have talked too long. This is a reminder that people value their time and do not want their time wasted.

## Team Time Management

Everyone on a team has a different approach to their work or project. A challenge for people is working as a team, which will change the

66 _Managing the Ministry_

process each team member utilizes for allotting time for their portion of the work. This can cause people to think they need to be more active, organized, and even overbearing. Each team will need to discuss how they approach their work or tasks when working together so everyone understands one another. The first step on a team is to organize the approach for achieving their desired outcome. Second, have team members express their approaches to their individual work. You could discuss different experiences and methods so the team can learn from one another. As the team works together, shared experiences will help cultivate a team mindset. Over time, the team can learn to anticipate and interpret expectations and challenges, improving support for one another. Teams should also develop principles of time stewardship and assist one another in using time well.

Managing a team's time is challenging when some units still need to develop a personal stewardship of time or a team member is established in his or her methods and is not open to more efficient approaches to ministry. You may have encountered an inflexible team member that is not open to change. As a leader, you must navigate the interpersonal relationships of the team members. Change is not easy for people when their process works for them. You will need to motivate and train toward a new paradigm for work and the time stewardship needed to benefit their life and ministry.

## Program Time Management

Programs should be managed to promote good time stewardship. If an event is planned and executed well, then time is optimized. Sometimes leaders are pushed or hurried and could be better prepared, leading to mismanagement of their team's time.

Break down a typical week for yourself with the understanding you need time for your spiritual habits, family, ministry, work, and holistic health. You understand that no two weeks are the same, although life often has rhythms. If you are trying to steward your time Sunday through Saturday with a fixed resource like time, then consider a stewardship plan. You take a development plan using a four-block day: morning, afternoon, evening, and night. Everyone has different schedules with start and end times for their work, so you can define these blocks in how you schedule them in six-hour blocks.

Consider the following example of a weekly rhythm through four daily blocks of time:

| DAY OF THE WEEK | BLOCK 1 | BLOCK 2 | BLOCK 3 | BLOCK 4 |
|---|---|---|---|---|
| SUNDAY | 6:00 am—12:00 pm | 12:00 pm—6:00 pm | 6:00 pm -12:00 am | 12:00 am—6:00 am |
| MONDAY | 6:00 am—12:00 pm | 12:00 pm—6:00 pm | 6:00 pm -12:00 am | 12:00 am—6:00 am |
| TUESDAY | 6:00 am—12:00 pm | 12:00 pm—6:00 pm | 6:00 pm -12:00 am | 12:00 am—6:00 am |
| WEDNESDAY | 6:00 am—12:00 pm | 12:00 pm—6:00 pm | 6:00 pm -12:00 am | 12:00 am—6:00 am |
| THURSDAY | 6:00 am—12:00 pm | 12:00 pm—6:00 pm | 6:00 pm -12:00 am | 12:00 am—6:00 am |
| FRIDAY | 6:00 am—12:00 pm | 12:00 pm—6:00 pm | 6:00 pm -12:00 am | 12:00 am—6:00 am |
| SATURDAY | 6:00 am—12:00 pm | 12:00 pm—6:00 pm | 6:00 pm -12:00 am | 12:00 am—6:00 am |

I have continued to craft my strategy with these blocks of time as my life rhythm changes, as I age, and as family dynamics change. Seasons of my life allowed me to stay up later when I was in college, and my work now requires an earlier start to the day. Scheduling blocks of time with intentionality will cause these blocks of your day to be stewarded with intentionality. You may need eight hours of sleep or have a determined shift time at work, so one of the four blocks of some days of your week must be extended. Some days might need blocks from 7:00am—12:00pm, 12:00pm—5:00pm, 5:00pm—10:00pm, and 10:00pm—7:00am. In each congregation, the people have different rhythms and schedules, and their time stewardship will vary. If we can increase time impact with a few tweaks, the lifelong impact with interest for investing time could be incredible.

### Questions to Consider

1. Do you have a healthy personal time stewardship approach?
2. What adjustments need to be made with program time management at your church?
3. How is overall ministry time stewardship being managed?
4. Pray over your stewardship and how you could leverage more time for the kingdom.

## Chapter 7:

# Metrics for Performance

S cripture teaches no two people are the same.[1] The unique nature of
each person must be considered in performance evaluation. Life
experiences, family origin, and generational influences impact work
performance and evaluation views. Generations approach work differently, leadership preferences vary by age, and approaches to loyalty
impact the local church. Millennials have changed the metrics as they
love their careers but easily change companies in search of promotions
and upward mobility. Their grandparents, however, may have only
worked for one company their whole careers. The diversity of unique
perspectives makes organizational management an ongoing challenge.

Picture the list you would create as you ponder life and work:
places to travel, life lessons to instill in your children, ministry milestones or spiritual markers to achieve, or non-negotiable operational
life values. Some of you reading this book may not be a list person and
desire to live in the moment. This challenges us because we approach
our life-work balance differently and have unique aspirations for living. You likely know someone that does not enjoy traveling far from
home and others that desire to see the world. In the church, it is hard

---

[1] Psalm 139.

to create metrics as we have a plurality of people that view life through different lens yet follow the same command to make disciples. As we seek to push back the darkness, teach, make devoted disciples, and multiply churches, we must consider the process of finding common ground to evaluate whether our work aligns with our mission, if our disciples reflect the Holy One, and if the ministry functions as intended. Do you prefer a prescribed standard or a realized outcome that aligns with the vision and mission? Your answer will guide the lens for reading this chapter. Some leaders desire everyone to follow the same standard that teaches the Bible the same way, and other leaders are content if the Bible is taught in different ways.

Every Sunday is busy. The church campus is full of people, with many volunteers making ministry happen. They have had a hectic week managing their lives, work, and family. While retirees might have a more flexible schedule, many families with school-age children have likely had full schedules of sports and extracurricular activities. They may have homeschooled or driven their kids to and from school, and now, after a crazy week, they land at their ministry assignment feeling pressed and perhaps confused. The staff team has similar life pressures, and overseeing all the ministries adds more stress that many do not understand. Metrics for reviewing performance is necessary. Assessment is a word that can make people grimace, and many do not enjoy assessing themselves or the organization. The people, property, programs, finances, and processes all need ongoing assessment in the church.

Academic environments utilize assessment to measure learning outcomes, program goals, and improvement strategies. Businesses use assessments for products, people, and results, looking for benchmarks, improvements, and weaknesses. The church should not be a place where we shy away from simple performance metrics to help improve processes, programs, and property that can aid in equipping for ministry. This does not have to be time consuming for leaders, but it must be an intentional process for review and dialogue. Metrics for performance are standard in business practice, allowing companies to measure new customer growth, current customer retention, and profit margin. While churches differ from most educational institutions or businesses, metrics are still needed for ministry alignment. For example, a simple financial metric assessment could be reviewing the church budget and income based on the previous three years.

Hopefully, your organization has a map of the organization and a plan for achieving the strategy. You may take the mission statement approach, develop objectives, and then create goals to accomplish the mission. Consider this concern: "fewer than one in ten organizations successfully execute their strategy because of some major barriers: the workforce doesn't understand the strategy, managers are not given the incentives to implement the strategy, executive teams don't discuss the strategy, and incredibly, their budgets are not well linked to their strategy."[2]

## Performance Feedback

How many people like unexpected feedback? You have heard stories of the varied comments a pastor receives about the sermon as people leave worship. Random comments on your clothes or hair may be exciting feedback. People project opinions toward you, your ministry, or the church by commenting on how they think things should be. Feedback is a fundamental metric for performance. Whether requested or volunteered, feedback helps ministry leaders gauge how things are going overall. It has been said that the loudest boos come from the cheapest seats, but this is not always true, as in the case of the Hellenistic Jews that were being left out in the distribution of food.[3] Sometimes the feedback loop is needed so ministry needs can be met and no one is left out. People, in general, can be caught off guard when they receive unexpected feedback, even when positive. Establishing metrics for performance reviews is a good way to give routine feedback and align intended ministry outcomes with current performance. Routine expected feedback creates a pathway for developing volunteers to meet established metrics. Gender can often affect performance reviews, where men are sometimes treated differently than women. In the workplace, men and women often have different wages and sometimes reviews for women focus on personality rather than their work, whereas men receive more feedback.[4] In the church, personnel

---

[2] George G. Babbes and Michael Zigarelli, *The Ministers MBA: Essential Business Tools for Maximum Ministry Success* (Nashville: B&H, 2006), 144.

[3] Acts 6:1.

[4] Carolina Aragão, "Gender Pay Gap in U.S. Hasn't Changed Much in Two Decades," Pew Research Center, March 1, 2023, https://www.pewresearch.org/short-reads/2023/03/01/gender-pay-gap-facts/.

committees tend to follow the patterns of the secular workplace with performance reviews.

Performance is a word often associated with automobiles, focusing on how they handle acceleration, move around the curves, and execute a drive with comfort and speed. A Shelby Mustang is expected to perform at high levels of speed. No one wants a car that barely cranks when they turn the key. A friend once picked me up in a new red Ferrari. I had never sat in a car of this level or cost before. The performance level was incredible and hard to describe. While it is just a vehicle that will get you from point A to point B, the ability of the vehicle is completely different from a car of lesser quality. I will never forget that drive and how the car handled the road. In ministry, we often just limp along more than performing at a high-level. Stress, burnout, or even the ongoing struggle of trying to lead against pushback cause discouragement for ministry leaders. In most organizations that rely on a volunteer structure, the challenge is measuring team execution by providing feedback through performance reviews. We need established standards for ministry so that we can review and tweak those standards in a way that increases performance quality. Stress and loneliness are growing among younger generations.[5] Their desire for ongoing feedback differs from older generations, who are no strangers to annual evaluations. Delivering assessments to other adults is challenging, with volunteers having varied attendance patterns. Paid staff can quickly provide feedback if the supervisor is willing to schedule the performance review regularly.

## Metrics for Performance

This chapter focuses on three metrics for ministry performance: property management, ministry programming, and business management. Performance could also be called execution or alignment to ministry objectives. Church members provide causal feedback as they talk about services, ministries, and people. Metrics take a more detailed approach. The first metric might seem unnecessary but should not be assumed for everyone. Ministry leaders are expected to walk with the Lord. They should cultivate spiritual habits through their daily lives. Metrics for staff and volunteers to grow in their relationship with Christ

---

[5] "Loneliness and Depression in Young Adults," Newport Institute, https://www.newportinstitute.com/resources/mental-health/loneliness-and-depression-young-adults/.

and walk with Christ should always be first. Chapter 13 is devoted to the formation of this vital area. However, a metric for performance is not intended to become a scorecard for spiritual habits.

A description for each volunteer position should be provided to help the congregation understand the expectations. Part of this process should recast the church's vision and demonstrate how the leader fits within the concept. This allows mission alignment to be a central part of the process to avoid gaps in alignment. A job description that provides a baseline for serving should be utilized for each position. The second important metric is established by these job descriptions as people are evaluated based on their alignment with established expectations clearly outlined, explained, and reviewed with each team member.

The third, more difficult, metric, is evaluating lifestyles within the congregation and outside scheduled church activities. This factor is not unique in light of the mission of the organization. Often people hire a great candidate on paper, but the person was not a cultural fit in the organization. The organizational culture is different between congregations. A great leader may have excelled in one organization but may not fit in another. Leaders may have incredible abilities but still need to find a better fit. A colleague conducted a study that discovered most ministerial staff members change within two years after a senior pastor change. The fit among staff, ministry leaders, congregations, and communities factors into leadership success. A second part of this metric is leaders' lives within families and outside communities. How one lives personally, when the church is not gathered together can be the least transparent. Society provides many ways to live a private life unknown to our closest family and friends. Often when something tragic happens, people respond that they would have never imagined it was possible. Even though false knowledge can be present, accountability can bring about conviction that leads to repentance in private areas of the ministry leader's life.

## Performance Evaluation

Performance is difficult for many people in ministry to evaluate. We do not create a panel of experts and rate each person like a reality TV competition even though having a "Church's Got Talent" to discern volunteer aptitudes would be amusing. People should not get a score but a review that helps them grow to be like Christ and increase their ministry effectiveness. Over my years in serving on church staff, the three metrics of property management, ministry programming, and business management were not expected but inspected by individual assumptions. I have had many evaluations based on job descriptions and performance with perceptions of execution, but I needed more feedback for property and business management. One key aspect is understanding that the metrics people employ are both formal and informal. Church members have many informal performance metrics in ministry based on their experiences or inherited expectations. People judge the style of preaching, dress code, demeanor, office hours, qualifications for lay leaders, and so on. Their expectations in these categories are often used to critique what they view as performance. Some people consider who speaks to them or how friendly they thought a person was when they happen to cross paths at church on one given Sunday, and this forms a critique based on that little encounter. This type of evaluation seemed to me an urban legend until it became apparent that some adults evaluate people based on limited interactions. The suggestion is to not go around a classroom shaking hands like someone running for elected office or work the worship room by moving throughout the sanctuary. Yet, ministry leaders must be aware that people are observing and drawing conclusions based on simple interactions each week or lack thereof. Position descriptions and codes of conduct for staff and lay leaders are crucial to help manage expectations of a diverse congregation with many opinions and experiences.

The Bible offers specific guidelines for several areas of the church. Offices of pastor, overseer, or elder have lists that have been used for generations to determine the metrics for who can serve in these roles. The office of deacon is also an area where specific guidelines are listed in the Bible for what qualifies a man to serve. The Bible also references the role of women serving in the church. Women serving in the church are vital to the overall ministry and work that needs to be accomplished. Every age group could not be ministered to without women's service through the local church. Most congregations will have a majority of female participants each week as they gather and offer ministry opportunities.[6]

---

[6] Aaron Earls, "Church Attendance Gender Gap Shrinks, but It's Not all Good News," *Lifeway Research*, September 25, 2017, https://research.lifeway.com/2017/09/25/church-attendance-gender-gap-shrinks-but-its-not-all-good-news/.

Each church will have guiding documents that outline the qualifications to serve in these various roles. The familiar places of children, students, women, and worship ministries are not the only places women desire to serve. Each congregation will need a clear understanding and process for how volunteers and paid leaders are selected and who can fill those roles. A rationale will need to be provided if women are not allowed to serve in certain areas of the church. This is not always clear because some denominations have tweaked common titles so that a person can fill a position that they otherwise could not. The title is a sticking point in evaluation for a lot of people. The issue of women teaching a co-ed adult or teenage group is one example where a church needs to have clearly defined qualifications. A biblical and theological rationale for positions, people, and processes will be required to provide clarity and evaluate the work being done in the specific role.

Metrics of performance and conduct for these roles should accompany guidelines to enable performance evaluation and aid in removing someone who no longer meets the biblical guidelines for the office they serve. Disciplinary processes for people who do not meet the standard for their position can be difficult. Performance coaching is another challenge in the church because no one likes being corrected. Being told how to change is typically uncomfortable to hear. Each church should have a discipline plan for church members in good standing. Additionally, a plan should be in place for correcting volunteers and staff members when their conduct does not meet the standards. Leaders must follow the plans for performance as they are established and not be selective in implementation. Drug use, sexual misconduct, social media misuse, or immoral internet activity are some specific areas of performance in which to execute stern discipline. Gluttony, gossip, and laziness are more difficult to enforce.

People are not the only area where metrics need to be established or clarified within the church. Earlier, we discussed the four foundational areas of property, programs, finances, and processes. Each of these areas touched on aspects of performance, but there a few specific things to note regarding metrics. Church property metrics should include a review of the cleanliness of an area each time it is occupied and how improvements can be made. You can establish standards for maintenance and check major systems for their performance. This allows leadership to know of possible future expenses or challenges.

Each scheduled program should be evaluated for achieving the intended objectives toward mission achievement. Established metrics can help leaders decide if an event or ongoing weekly program needs to be reimagined, replaced, or eliminated. Data can help inform hard decisions and show why a change is necessary. Financial metrics can help the organization know if giving has increased or decreased, if income is up, or if expenses are down. Data sets that aid in evaluating the fiscal portfolio each year are essential for leaders. Some may feel that this data removes reliance on the Lord's provision, but it can provide historical information about giving and how the church's people respond. Only some processes or systems that have been developed and implemented actually function as intended or assist the organization as planned. Evaluating processes in a changing culture is vital to reveal if they cover the original scope or need to be tweaked for new realities or challenges. These review areas should indicate a healthy organization that is achieving its mission and handling its challenges effectively.

A few words of caution about utilizing metrics for performance: no one person will be perfect every day with every encounter and with every person. If a person has an area that needs improvement, mentor them to improve. Some people do not realize that a person may not speak to others in the hall because they are still processing from their teaching time or pondering a conversation as they leave their ministry assignment en route to the next stop on Sunday. Extroverts and introverts may have different mindsets on interactions with people, even if they have the same spiritual gifts. People's natural inclinations for personality, leadership, and gifting can help create ministry leaders' profiles. Metrics are vital because people need to know the challenges to overcome as they grow to be more like Christ. As feedback is given in a positive way to produce growth, the church benefits from stronger members and leaders.

### Questions to Consider

1. Do you have prescribed metrics for evaluating those serving in ministry positions at your church?
2. How do you like to receive feedback that will help you grow in your relationship with Christ?
3. What are ways that metrics can be used in a negative or hurtful way? How can you avoid using metrics in those ways?

4. People are renewed when they receive positive feedback. How can you be intentional in providing ongoing positive feedback as you observe strengths in others?

# Chapter 8:

# Workflow Solutions

J acob is a husband, father, and minister. Each week he tries to make it all work. A sermon, a minimum of two teaching times, and a weekly staff meeting devotion and agenda all need to be prepped for delivery. He needs to glance over the financials, make one-on-one time for a few staff members, and visit several families in crisis. This is just what is known in a standard weekly schedule for ministers. But ministry does not stop with the standard items on a schedule. A struggling couple may need a call of encouragement. Volunteer ministry group leaders may need to be checked on as they follow up with guests and reach out to one another. This leader works full-time with a family and tries to find solutions for his church, family, and business rhythm. Similarly, church volunteers have many demands on their time. The small group leader may have an overnight work trip or important client meetings regarding future work all in the same week. A volunteer may have regular ministry leaders' meetings, daily office and family schedules, and weekly prepping and teaching of lessons. Pastors, small group leaders, deacons, and staff members have different stressors and challenges, but one common thread is the busy pace of life where everyone seeks solutions to accomplish the work each week.

Life and work seem to be getting harder for most people who feel like they are running from one event, errand, or engagement to another without enough time. Others are trying to figure out a home and office balance that allows them to feel that they can complete their work without extending into evenings and weekends. Businesses are now dealing with a workflow situation that ministers and volunteers in the church have lived with for centuries. The work is an ongoing process in the church as we strive to fulfill the mission. However, people do need rest and margin so that they can replenish. It was predicted that work would decrease and leisure would increase by this generation, yet people are working to maintain their status and positions more than ever.[1] God created everything in six days and then rested. A healthy balance of pressing forward yet having a day of rest and release is the rhythm presented to us in the early chapters of Genesis.

In a generation where technology and efficiency are recurring themes in the workplace, the ministry must consider what work solutions fit the church context. At the same time, a biblical process toward work and ministry must be maintained. This may be the most challenging aspect of managing an organization. The three primary areas of people, property, and programs inform systems that these areas rely upon, but the struggle is the fluidity of these three. They are constantly changing, thus, changing the solutions to the work in an ongoing continuum. J. Daryl Charles observed that

> there is a vastly compelling need for resources that will enable pastors, priests, educators, Christian leaders, and indeed laypersons themselves to cultivate a vision for (1) the design and dignity of work, (2) the importance of the doctrine of vocation, and (3) the high calling of the workplace. After all, this is where we believers spend much of our lives and can best influence society.[2]

The church is in a season of understanding the workflow of its people, property, program, finances, and processes. These are ongoing tasks that have recently garnered more focus due to outlying factors impacting established rhythms. Ministers must keep in mind that as they struggle to figure out their workflow, so do the leaders around them.

---

[1] Cam Marston, *Motivating the "What's In It for Me?" Workforce,* (Hoboken: John Wiley & Sons, 2007), 122.

[2] J. Daryl Charles, *Our Secular Vocation* (Brentwood, TN: B&H Academic, 2023), 15.

The church should be a place to equip the people to work well in their environments to impact people for Christ.

## Digital Workflow Solutions

The digital world has caused people to have many different approaches to their work. Ministry has limits to the extent digital solutions can provide for the position. People need interaction, and while digital aids can provide information without an in-person meeting, the prep may require even more time. Digital solutions may involve more team members to create, edit, and distribute content. In modern staff meetings, there may be people of various ages with multiple types of screens in front of them. One person may have an annual paper-bound planner, some use tablets with multiple calendars and task lists apps, and some come with just a notepad. This snapshot organization reminds us that different ages and personality styles approach work differently.

We could spend much time exploring various apps that can help our work, but the focus of this chapter will be looking at the administrative advantages and solutions available to manage organizations and their systems. Various apps can be workflow tools to take your productivity anywhere you want at work or at home. It is convenient for many to have a digital work platform wherever they may be. It also comes with a cost because when work is readily available, it never stops.

In his book *Atomic Habits*, James Clear reveals that small incremental changes to our habits can profoundly impact individuals and organizations. The math of a simple tiny improvement shows, "If you can get 1 percent better each day for one year, you'll end up thirty-seven times better by the time you're done. Conversely, if you get 1 percent worse each day for one year, you'll decline nearly down to zero. What starts as a small win or a minor setback accumulates into something much more."[3] As you administer the work in your organization, you may want dramatic changes or noticeable wins, which is understandable. A small group leader desires to see transformation. The worship pastor expects to see people worshipping as they gather each week. A student minister wants to see the numbers increase. In each area of the church, leaders desire noticeable growth and wins in the work they give their life to each week. A simple approach to the work is not reaching for dynamic wins

---

[3] James Clear, *Atomic Habits* (New York: Avery, 2018), 15.

but committing to the work the Lord has given you each day and looking for 1 percent growth in your leadership and ministry.

## Team Workflow Solutions

There are ways to make simple tweaks to ongoing functioning of a team, which will improve the workflow for your people. Take time to examine the systems and work that needs to be accomplished, and noticeable improvement and efficiency can be realized throughout a church year. Janitorial staff can continually look for daily ways to improve their work and the approaches taken to achieve each task. When first impressions ministry volunteers routinely examine how to be good teammates, the overall ministry improves as individual team members' habits improve. I consult at many churches and am amazed at how many of the greeters, ushers, or first impressions are not friendly nor engaging. My observations reveal that most people catch up with people they know or desire to talk to and let the guests pass by or flag them down to get a worship guide. This is just one example. If the church provided training aimed at improvement solutions for intentional improvement each week, the impact over time would be significant. This logic can be applied to all areas of service in the church.

Training is an area that can reinvigorate people for ministry or bore them into surfing social media or checking the score of a sporting event. The purpose of trainings is to equip our people to lead in their respective areas of ministry. Minor tweaks can help people move their church forward with simple tools or habits that they can employ to improve their work in ministry.

Meetings can be pointless, where everyone rolls their eyes and laments that it could have just been an email. These meetings are typically informational, not engaging or requiring input. A clear agenda and purpose is needed for each meeting, and those invited should be the right people for the meeting's purpose.

## Meetings and Communication

What comes to mind when you think of meetings? Ponder your last three meetings. Were they productive? Do the diverse members of your team perceive meetings differently? Hopefully, your people do not share the sentiment of a coffee mug I saw, "I survived another meeting that could have been an email." While the mug could have been created by a Gen Xer working for a novelty company that puts sarcastic expressions on various items, sentiments about meetings are usually not positive. Many approaches exist to improve your meetings. One easy tweak is to follow an agenda, with an efficient point person who can run the meeting and keep people focused. Meetings should have a purpose. If you have a weekly meeting just because it is on the calendar, younger generations on your team will multitask during the staff meeting. Your agenda can set the tone, pace, and purpose of your meeting. Review previous agendas to understand the scope and purpose of prior meetings to help you decide what to include in upcoming meetings.

Another thing to consider is the meeting length. During the COVID-19 pandemic, some pastors instituted the forty-minute staff meeting, which came about in response to online platforms that allowed forty minutes of meeting time without a paid subscription. This can be an efficient and specific way to execute a team meeting. What are some ways you could improve as you think about the meetings you schedule, manage, and lead?

Input and communication are crucial aspects of a meeting. If a leader desires team buy-in, all members should be allowed to share input. Allowing others to give feedback, share ideas, and offer insights from their perspectives is a must. We have all likely experienced a meeting where input was not desired from the team or communication was one way. Meetings where people are not allowed to participate will lead to less engagement, and members will eventually find their work not life-giving. People desire to steward their time, talent, and treasure in the church. They desire a structure that allows input and communication around their values. A system that wastes resources is not productive for the organization.

The organization's structure will determine who attends meetings, but workflow solutions determine the existing committees and teams in the church. The structure will then configure the workflow or bureaucracy of the church. Many churches have a congregational structure, meaning members have influence and the ability to vote on significant factors with people, property, programs, and finances. Meetings are crucial to this structure because committees and teams will determine the flow of information to congregational meetings. This creates one system in the church, which informs meetings, information, communication, and organization to accomplish the work.

# Organization Structure Impact on Workflow Solutions

Another strategy that needs consideration deals with the property and the workflow required to manage the physical plant. Chapter five outlined processes within the organization, along with systems that help people achieve their work. Some of these are simple, yet not all of the systems are normally followed by all types of people in the church.

Many may have a love-hate relationship with church software because we need to know the information of our people with contact, family members, and the areas they serve. We utilize systems like this for event registration, guest registration, membership data, financial records, and pastoral care. Churches may have just one software system for all these functions or several. A church may utilize one system for financials and another for people. Apps also exist as part of some systems, while other churches have developed an app specifically for their needs.

# Organizational Management Impact on Workflow Solutions

HVAC, security, RFID door access, and other facility systems offer solutions for managing the buildings and improving security and safety for the organization. Numerous business solutions are available to help your organization as you manage these areas. You can partner with a company that manages HVAC systems and offers routine maintenance contracts. A security company that offers RFID configuration for entry points throughout the facility could also provide a security system with surveillance for your organization. Janitorial companies offer many services to help you with all aspects of your cleaning needs, from floors to bathrooms. We all desire to walk into a space that smells refreshing and clean. Just imagine a restaurant or hotel that did not pass the test. I stayed at a national chain hotel recently that did not pass the clean standard that the company claims. The room needed to be cleaned before another guest arrived. We do not want our strained systems or workflows to display a ministry that is not prepared. The struggle with workflow solutions and first impressions is not to overburden people or create a secular culture but to care for people.

Workflow solutions can be helpful for staff that struggles with meeting project deadlines. Tools are only as beneficial as people's willingness to learn how to use them effectively. The team must understand that solutions can be utilized in different ways but still accomplish the same objective. For example, someone may organize email folders for productivity or files on their computer differently than you but still manage to work effectively. If a solution requires conformity by everyone, productivity can be diminished.

## Leader's Impact on Workflow Solutions

Are you a problem solver? Do people consider you to be one that is tweaking work solutions constantly? You have probably worked with someone who enjoyed trying to find a better solution to how a project or process was going. You may be the person that likes to refine and improve systems. However, many adults want to dream, wonder, or cast an idea forward and are drained by considering ways to improve. They are not wired to find an improved workflow. This is a popular topic in many organizations because the world is changing so fast that people cannot keep up their current pace. The stress and anxiety expressed even among children have caused leaders to realize they have to find a better path forward to create life margins outside of simply working on task completion. People are one aspect of time, but the programs rely on a system to solve their weekly workflow.

We look for a better workflow to create a margin for what matters most. My rationale is simple: I desire to spend more time in spiritual habits and with my family. Ministry is a love for me, and I leverage my life toward ministry. However, my top two priorities are my relationship with Jesus and my family. I should not be consumed with text messages, emails, meetings, and preparation for the next thing. God has impressed two things upon me—to love him and my family. The rest falls in line. The solution for the Christian is to free up more time with God, family, ministry, and his church. You may be a paid staff member or know of one who feels like they can never take time off. You might also know a volunteer that feels they must be at church constantly. Dedication is an important aspect of serving at church, but if any leader is out on Sunday, most churches will still meet and carry on. No one is indispensable, which makes equipping the saints essential to the work.

Time and how it is tracked for employees can be challenging. Some positions need a straightforward solution to improve workflow. Many aspects are seasonal. A children's ministry team leader will have a busier spring and summer, whereas the worship leader may have a more active fall into spring with Christmas and Easter. Many church members know the schedules and work patterns within their ministry areas. The personnel team will need to seek input from the ministry areas, not just a secular job performance metric, to consider improving workflow. A ministry assistant may work better with children's ministry and worship ministry because of the complimentary seasons within the two ministries. Each church needs to consider the organization's workflow and how the work is assigned, leading to a system for organizational improvement. If a few training sessions on productivity and time management will help many on the team then the more significant challenge is the calendaring the execution of the work with people, property, and programs.

Some items in a church can consume time and bandwidth for work in ministry. One of those areas is food service. A Wednesday night meal, food for bereavement, and special events can drain time with set-up, food preparation, and clean-up. This area of organizational management should be delegated to capable people who can lead, equip, and execute effectively.

Office hours in a new church require reconsidering the philosophy of the church office, as detailed in chapter five. The workflow of the office is different as more adults communicate and give digitally and more adults are occupied during office daytime hours.

Everything in church ministry does not always happen as planned. Somedays, you will realize that something unexpected needs to be completed, messing up your workflow. Other times, you invest countless hours for a lackluster attendance to an event. People are last minute to sign up and only sometimes forthright or committed to their responsibilities.

The goal for workflow is twofold: (1) find things that need to be completed and (2) have the margin to forecast and anticipate the work in your area so you can lead, delegate, or motivate the team to accomplish the work. Andy Andrews stated it best with these words:

> If you and I are to become extraordinary achievers, we must learn to recognize the little things that create the gap—and, consequently, the difference in opportunities—between one and two. Astonishingly, these little things that most people see as irrelevant sometimes occur days or weeks before the event. And know this: the difference is

in the little things because the actual gap between first and second place is most often ridiculously small.[4]

As you consider workflow solutions, pay attention to those small habits, tweaks, or details because the difference, as observed in athletics, is usually a slight gain in the race, game, or competition. Paul utilizes the theme of running the race or competing in battle by enforcing discipline upon the individual:

> Don't you know that runners in a stadium all race, but only one receives the prize? Run in such a way to win the prize. Now everyone who competes exercises self-control in everything. They do it to receive a perishable crown, but we an imperishable crown. So, I do not run like one who runs aimlessly or box like one beating the air. Instead, I discipline my body and bring it under strict control, so that after preaching to others, I myself will not be disqualified.[5]

Paul reminds the reader that everyone is training and competing with self-control in all things. Running with a mission requires discipline and focus. The workflow plan you adopt should not distract you from the discipline to remain qualified for the work. If you have many difficulties in your organization or struggle to find a starting place for yourself, your team, and your congregation, consider bringing in an outside perspective. Hiring a consultant for your organization can help people see through a different lens. A new perspective for people, property, and programs can help the leadership cultivate the congregation to enhance their collective work. Sometimes the process reveals some things that need to be eliminated. During a season with a consultant, areas are discovered that need to be expanded.

### Questions to Consider

1. Does the training your organization provides need to be tweaked or digitized?
2. Do you need help leading or managing meetings? Why?
3. Do support ministry areas like food service drain resources or provide a needed ministry?

---

[4] Andy Andrews, *The Little Things: Why You Should Really Sweat the Small Stuff* (Nashville: Thomas Nelson, 2017), 4.

[5] 1 Cor 9:24–27.

## Chapter 9:

# Risk Factors

Parents from different eras approach safety in various ways. Some reading this book enjoyed family vacations while driving unbuckled in the back of a station wagon, just relaxing and having a great time. You may remember riding along in the bed of a truck, having a great summer ride with no thought of what could go wrong. You might be one of the kids with a house full of plastic plug covers and cabinet closures, who never unloaded the dishwasher and always rode in an age-appropriate car seat. Culture has shifted toward creating safe environments at home and everywhere children interact with the world. Today that focus has shifted again to consider security due to active shooters and violence at schools and churches. You may be questioning why a book like this needs a chapter on risk factors. Because the world has become more dangerous and people have access to news in real-time, many desire more security. Families bring these thoughts to church and every aspect of ministry. This does not mean ministry leaders should overreact, but they should be aware of the need to have fresh eyes on your property, people, and processes. In this chapter, we will explore topics that need to be considered by congregations as they create safety protocols and response plans for their church.

I have fond memories of my childhood, and thankfully, no one was significantly injured as we created forts, rode three- and four-wheelers, and devised all kinds of schemes and mischievous activities that have grown in severity as they are retold through an adult lens. In all transparency, I would not desire for my kids to engage in the same adventures because one less emergency room visit would be nice, but I do hope for my kids to enjoy the journey. They need to have great adventures and memories, but I also want them to be safe. Over the years, a culture of safety awareness has emerged as adults become more conscious of their kids' online and in-person environments. Anytime the word risk comes up, some naturally roll their eyes while others think the worst-case scenarios still need to be fully explored. A few common terms ministry leaders need to consider when discussing risk with congregations include avoidance, transfer, reduced, shared, and residual. These are the lens to use to evaluate each regular ministry and special event.

"Avoiding" could mean canceling an event because the risk is too great. A Thanksgiving turkey shoot, common in the South, could be an event to cancel in today's environment for safety and security. A "transfer" is where the risk is not on behalf of the congregation but transferred to another party. Utilizing a retreat center for a "Disciple NOW" event instead of people's homes would transfer (not eliminate) risk to another entity. "Reducing" risk is what most congregations find themselves doing. For example, by removing clutter and problems in their facility, they are reducing the possible risks as people gather. "Sharing" risk is when your church partners with other churches or associations, and you share the risk as a plurality of organizations. "Residual" risks are where you make your building available to others outside your organization. You will have some liability because the other organization has insurance related to your property, but you still have some risk exposure. These are examples of the significant ways an insurance company considers your risk, which helps guide our thinking as we strive to create safer environments for ministry and more secure congregations as we gather.

Another aspect that should be explored is how to conduct a risk assessment for churches and their ministries. Analyzing possible risk factors will inform leaders how to avoid, transfer, reduce, share, or consider future residual factors for the organization through their people, property, program, and finances.

Research on risk factors has revealed adults are more concerned with safety as it relates to their kids.[1] The content for classes I teach in this area includes news articles about safety missteps by churches. Recent news in just one day revealed a minister fined by the IRS for not reporting all his income, a church scammed out of hundreds of thousands of dollars during a building project, and a historic church raising money to restore their facility. If you are still skeptical of this topic, explore Church Law and Tax and scroll through the various reports of issues with churches.[2] In my work with churches, I interpret potential risks among paid staff and volunteers, properties, and finances. Risk factors expand into everything with people, property, and programs. My office receives several calls a week from churches or ministry leaders who need help to navigate a concern. During this process, I outline potential risks and problems for churches to help us be on the same page. Each risk that I explore with churches is based on a true occurrence in a local church. These concepts are not fictional aspects that are dreamed up for what could happen but are addressed in light of what has happened and how congregations and their people could be better equipped to prepare for, navigate, and respond to risk factors. This discussion reminds my clients that we cannot eliminate risk, but we can plan, evaluate, and prepare so we have safer ministries and stronger processes to respond when something occurs.

Churches have a raised awareness of risk factors as they continue seeing the rise of gun violence in schools and churches. Places of learning and worship should be safe and secure, but the environment can become hostile or threatened by people inside or outside. Although the chances are still very slim for a violent security threat at church, many churches have men who feel the need to be aware and provide a secure campus. Church shootings have increased in recent decades, so it is more of a risk than ever. This concern has caused some to take on church security as their personal mission, but this is misguided if discipleship of those serving is not factored into the process. I have observed many men who stand watch but never reach a pew or small

---

[1] Rob Gabriele, "Report on Parenting in America," SafeHome.org, August 23, 2022, https://www.safehome.org/family-safety/parenting-in-america-report/.

[2] *Christianity Today's* website "Church Law and Tax" (https://www.churchlawandtax.com) is an excellent resource to help churches with legal issues, tax aspects, ministers, property, ministry with minors, insurance, governance, liability, and finances are just a few areas that this tool provides to help organizations and leaders in this area.

group. They are committed to being present but not involved. Ministry leaders must develop a plan for the spiritual formation and worship of their safety and security team.

## Safety and Security

Churches should consider several aspects and assign members of the security team to be responsible for safety with minors and adults, safety and security with property, programming safety through church ministries, and protection of finances. These areas have unique challenges and risk factors, which should be reflected in a risk management plan.

People in ministry, whether children, teenagers, adults, or senior adults, have safety challenges. The primary concerns with minors are safety while under the ministry care and well-being in their homes. Sexual misconduct and other abuse can happen in the home, and the church is one place where ministry leaders may notice evidence of physical or emotional abuse. The elderly are also vulnerable to abuse, and signs are noticeable in retirement home ministries or with regular church attendance. The need to protect minors from harm has risen to the forefront as issues of sexual misconduct have continued to be revealed across denominations. Although we know people will never be perfect, we do desire to provide a safe environment where people within the church can be trusted. While churches need to increase security and safety processes, there is also a need to be a people of love who are not continuously profiling every sneeze, smile, or snicker. Sexual abuse is not the only safety challenge a congregation faces, but it is the most discussed in recent years.

Another safety area for all ages is their well-being while on the property. From the parking lot to the chair, and any stop in between, have safety needs because people are involved. Anyone can resolve issues in the parking lot by making people aware of concerns and creating safeguards. The more significant challenge is a thorough screening process to recruit paid and volunteer staff for all areas of service. This is one of the more sensitive areas to try and address in an organization because it is personal for everyone. You will have people who desire to approach church security like that of a military base, while others avoid discussing the problems at all. Some believe screening is necessary for everyone but themselves. As churches raise awareness of the need to establish policies with children and students, leaders will start to question motives or feel like the focus is on outsiders rather than those already working in church. As these conversations grow, the reality is that many assume church is a safe environment and believe that issues beyond someone having an accident or a medical emergency are minimal risks for ministry because they cannot conceive of a family member or a church member they know harming a minor. The one question I have pondered for years in my service to churches is why we spend thousands of dollars on property insurance for the building but are difficult and stingy when it comes to protecting our kids and vetting the people that serve them.

A background check costs a few dollars per person, yet some congregations and ministry leaders are hesitant to invest in this most basic screening tool for staff. Inviting a leader to come in and conduct a training weekend for risk with people is more expensive but doable, especially if churches partner together, but equipping the people to serve within the church is needed. I may not have always been required to wear a seatbelt as a kid, but faithful adults policed the rules that were needed at the time to keep us safe at church and school. At church, adults took responsibility for the collective whole of kids. Back then, we were only occasionally the most manageable group to corral. Adults were faithful to attend services, serve in ministries, participate in business meetings, and engage in training events. That season of ministry was very different than it is today. The world has changed, and ministry culture and expectations have shifted to a place where safety is a high priority. Hayrides and bonfires were annual events in the past, without much thought of what could go wrong. For most churches, discipleship-focused weekends and retreats did not include planning for how to deal with bullying, peer-on-peer abuse, or adult misconduct. Extended families used to surround their senior adult family members within walking or driving distance and would routinely check on them. As shifts happen in ministry cultures, the annual events, weekly ministry opportunities, and new ideas need to be considered through a new safety lens. A list of things to consider for the physical safety of your people should include medical or weather emergencies. Severe weather is often not considered in our physical safety plans at our church buildings. People need to know how to respond to a weather emergency event when present on the church property.

## Property Concerns

Risk factors with property exist because the church owns land and buildings. On any given day, someone can be injured. Scheduled events have some risk exposure as people are invited onto the property for a planned purpose. An accident resulting from dim lighting, a crack in the sidewalk, or a missed step on the stairs can happen anywhere. Simple accidents are easy to understand and will likely be a minor issue that the organization's insurance, along with the individual's health insurance, can cover. More significant issues that rise to the attention of a billboard lawyer's radar is when a severe accident occurs due to negligence on the part of the organization. For example, a pavilion lost structural integrity from years of use and weather, and it was known it needed repair. During an event, the pavilion collapsed on people, and many were injured. The most common risk factor for properties is the potential for injury while someone is on the premises.

Classrooms, offices, closets, kitchens, meeting spaces, fellowship halls, sanctuaries, restrooms, sidewalks, and playgrounds are just a few areas of risk within the property. Risk concerns are present as long as people have access to places to serve. For example, kids should not have access to offices or a kitchen. You may have members who think that they should have keys to the entire facility. This is a challenge as the focus on safety and security has increased with the rise of active shootings, mental health concerns, and the overall decline of trust among adults. Since minors gather in various areas of the building, we must think like a school that limits outside access to minors. Conversely, worship spaces need a security plan that follows large event protocols.

## Programs: Sports, Events, Weekly Planned Events

Risk factors with people never end because we cannot read the minds of others. Each church should conduct background checks, enforce a screening process for staff and volunteers, and require training for everyone. This system is still flawed because we live in a fallen world. People can still do many things in private that the church and its leaders may not know about. Television dramas, though many fictional, highlight how twisted the world can be and how people quietly execute evil acts. Thankfully, a low percentage of churches experience the worst-case scenario risks, but the need to take the utmost care in protecting people remains. Simple tweaks to your processes with people, property upgrades, and program understandings can reduce risk quickly. The most minor tweaks can improve safety as people understand and are equipped with skills and knowledge on how to react when something occurs.

Generational differences, policies and procedures, and people are challenges in a changing church culture and are amplified in the polarizing world we find ourselves navigating. A negative news story in a community about one congregation causes many people to think differently about all congregations in their community to some degree. This unfortunate climate requires the organization to communicate with families about safety measures and missional reasons for our programming.

Issues surrounding gender fluidity create many obstacles to ministry in the church. Society has shifted toward a gender choice approach which allows parents and children to choose the gender, thus creating several risk factors emotionally, physically, mentally, and spiritually. Each organization must decide how the issue of gender will be handled, as children and adults are a part of the church that may have gender challenges in their lives. This is an evolving aspect of risk management for the church and will continue to add factors for ministry and organizational consideration.

If you do not consider risk factors with minors an issue, then consider the preschools, elementary, and secondary schools in your community. They have plans for fire, severe weather, transportation, and facilities. People are screened before they are allowed to work with children. The entire process considers safety and security. They do not always get it right, but they consistently strive to be as safe and secure as possible. Could the church model that level of care for the community and become a place where training is valued, and people know minors are safe? The challenge to issues in a changing culture is when an organization is already behind in safety and security and the effort and time needed to implement safety strategies are compounded with ongoing ministry needs. Considering several years of news cycles that reveal adult misconduct in churches, it is likely that parents are increasingly aware that a problem could exist.

My family understands the church and school side of the conversation because we have been on staff in organizations when staff, teacher, and minister misconduct occurred with a minor or adult. Whether or not each issue could have been avoided is a matter of speculation; however, people suffered because of misconduct. Minister or volunteer misconduct must be taken seriously.

Programming risk factors include people and property since it is impossible to have ministry programming without people leading and volunteering to serve through those programs. Each ministry needs a place and resources, which involve the church's property or an extension of the church property through another location, usually a church member's home. Sometimes a local business will serve as a connecting spot for mentoring or discipleship with smaller groups. Ministries to local first responders, hospitals, schools, and nursing homes are areas that churches serve through outreach and support. Ministry programming also happens at parks, apartment complexes, and community events as the church supports children's enrichment programs. A comprehensive list of all the possibilities would include examples of unique recreation, discipleship, missions, or music programming for ministry locally, regionally, or internationally. When you leave your property for an event in the community, a retreat out of town, or another place on mission, the same risk factors follow you wherever you go. Risk factors can expand since more aspects beyond our established systems have yet to be discovered as we are around fewer familiar facilities or people. Risk factors should not cause us to strive to do less in ministry but help us consider how we can be as safe and secure as possible.

## Steps to Create a Risk or Incident Response Plan

Negligence is a word used in the medical field or child services when a person is not given a standard of care that should have been provided. A church also has a standard of care that people expect when ministry opportunities are made available to people, especially minors.

A few words of caution are in order here. Each congregation must evaluate its risks and provide a safe and secure environment for ministry. Plans for risk vary from church to church,, but each area should be addressed. Jesus asked us to care for and reach people and be lights in our communities; trust must be established. Some people will question every aspect of the plan, while others will think it is a waste of time. This is one area of organizational management that people will only sometimes understand. Yet, people will ask why more was not done to prevent harm when something happens. Due diligence is required in this area. As questions arise, the church and its people should understand that best practices are in place and leaders are equipped to do all they can to reduce, avoid, share, or transfer the risk.

### Questions to Consider

1. Do you have standards in place to protect and provide a safe and secure environment for all your work with minors? Does this include standards for volunteers?
2. Does the church have a vetting process for vendors or partners, whether an on-site event or venue off campus?
3. Do the people in your church who serve as mandatory reporters know the standards in your state and other regions where members may travel and how to execute that requirement?
4. Gender fluidity is an evolving issue from children to adults. What policies need to be in place to help families understand the church's stance? How does the organization deal with volunteers, outside events, trips for ministry, weddings, or funerals?
5. Do you have plans for a security threat on campus during an event or worship service?
6. Does the church have severe weather and fire plans that include shelter and evacuation routes posted throughout the facility?

Note: This is not a comprehensive chapter on all the risk factors or how to execute each aspect to the highest standard. Instead, this chapter is a ministry introduction to risk factor considerations for your church and leaders. Please take the time to explore this area further and have straightforward prevention and reaction plans for these areas of concern.

## Chapter 10:

# Generational Differences

We live in exciting times. We have at least five generations of different experiences and views that come together as one in the church. An organization may not have all five, but it is highly possible that your church will have at least three adult generations striving to serve together. My grandfather and I were inseparable when I was a kid as we worked on the house, garage, barn, land, and pond. I loved being in his shadow while we tinkered with machines, repaired houses, or worked on the land, especially when it meant I got to drive a tractor. My unique relationship with my grandparents gave me a genuine love for older adults. As I aged and could drive, I would visit various older adults from church on my way home from school. I remember many conversations about church, studying the Bible, the different changes they had observed in life and church, and how to be faithful with what you have, no matter how little or much it may be. My experiences may be unique, but I wanted to share them because if we are willing to find ways to spend time together, the shared wisdom and understanding between generations is remarkable.

We see this in the Old Testament when a leader chooses not to consult the younger generation or when a group is not considered in decision making. As a result, the consequences of those limited views caused problems. We will always have preferences and differences as people join together to be the church. The church is a family that should have a seat at the table for everyone who enters and lets them know they are welcome. The New Testament also reveals generational challenges, with Jesus choosing the twelve from the larger group of disciples. These young men did not always agree and asked various questions that showed their desire for authority, such as who would get to sit on Jesus's right and left. Paul had many challenges throughout his missionary journey. The famous debate over the younger John Mark, causing Barnabas and Paul to part ways, reveals generational differences and approaches to the work. Both paths were understandable, and Barnabas and Paul had great ministries and were great leaders. Sometimes, differences will cause us to better serve the kingdom by moving to a different place of service. The letters Paul sent to the churches reveal differences that people had with culture, age, and spiritual maturity. Adults would be well served by reading the wisdom found in Psalms and Proverbs daily. We have wise counsel on how to live and respect both young and older adults around us.

Paul discussed spiritual gifts several times, but First Corinthians has a detailed listing of spiritual gifts and a discussion of the body of Christ and its unity. In this description of the body, Paul described various parts and provided the reader a vivid illustration that the body needs each piece, no matter what its gifts, to be a complete body. In the words of Paul from 1 Cor 12:12–26:

> For just as the body is one and has many parts and all the parts of that body, though many, are one body—so also is Christ. For we were all baptized by one Spirit into one body—so also is Christ. For we were all baptized by one Spirit into one body—whether Jews or Greeks, whether slaves or free—and we were all given one Spirit to drink. Indeed, the body is not one part but many. If the foot should say, "Because I'm not a hand, I don't belong to the body," it is not for that reason any less a part of the body. And if the ear should say, "Because I'm not an eye, I don't belong to the body," it is not for that reason any less a part of the body. If the whole body were an eye, where would the hearing be? If the whole body were an ear, where would the sense of smell be? But as it is, God has arranged each one of the parts in the body just as he wanted. And if they were all the same part, where would the body be? As it is, there are many parts, but one body. They eye cannot say to the hand, "I don't need

you!" Or again, the head can't say to the feet, "I don't need you!" On the contrary, those parts of the body that are weaker are indispensable. And those parts of the body that we consider less honorable, we clothe these with greater honor, and our unrespectable parts are treated with greater respect, which our respectable parts do not need. Instead, God has put the body together, giving greater honor to the less honorable, so that there would be no division in the body, but that the members would have the same concern for each other. So, if one member suffers, all the members suffer with it, if one member is honored, all the members rejoice with it.

Each person is valuable within the body, meaning people of all ages are needed in the congregation. A younger person is not waiting to be a part of a future church, and a senior adult has not retired from being needed in the church. As ministry leaders, it is critical to understand the value and needs of each person. Discovering the gifts and abilities of members is a needed part of equipping people to serve in the various ministries of the church. Each body part has a unique function that together serves to help us move, hear, smell, taste, and see. Some parts are challenged by our health and struggles in this world, and, if you are one of those, do not be discouraged by this discussion. In the body, there are ways for each person to serve and make themselves useful. There have been some strong prayer warriors for the church that could not leave their homes due to their health and mobility.

The body of Christ also needs each person to serve with a unified spirit in the Lord. If you have worked with other people, then you know whether in a classroom, assembly line, or an office, conflict with others can be difficult to avoid as we approach our work and abilities from different angles and perspectives, putting strain on relationships. Haydn Shaw's research has revealed some ways we can understand one another and work together with a more unified work ethic as we serve the Lord.[1] The principles can be applied in the workplace but also have application to the local church. As people age, various aspects impact the way they view the world. Their lens has been cultivated through traditions, and their conscience has developed thoughts that may be more rooted in tradition than Scripture. Shaw explores the

---

[1] Haydn Shaw, *Sticking Points: How to Get Five Generations Working Together in the 12 Places They Come Apart,* (Carol Stream, IL: Tyndale Momentum, 2020), 12.

challenges facing the five adult generations that are attempting to do life together as they interact with one another.

Shaw's writing on the various adult generations and how they can come together or blow apart in twelve key areas have great application for the church. Experience in the local church reveals that this research on different generations working together can also apply to the church and the people. What is simple to some can be non-negotiable for others. His research indicates that while each person differs on issues, the twelve most common that he addresses help teams move forward together: "If the five generations will acknowledge the twelve sticking points and work through them as a team, they will find themselves liberated to become a team with a unified vision instead of a group with different agendas. Instead of generational differences holding your team back, these differences will become the fuel that propels your team forward."[2] You may be pondering which five generations we are considering. They are the Traditionalists, Baby Boomers, Generation Xers, Millennials, and Gen Zers, which make up the adult outlook in the church. Your church will have a different blend of these groups of people.

As you understand the average age of the people in your church, you can consider the aging process as new people come and your older adults are no longer available. Over time, one of the most challenging aspects of ministry is remembering a dear servant who was special to the church's work and is now in heaven. I have had the blessing of some dear prayer warriors, Bible teachers, chaperones, and partners in the ministry. Many could be listed. However, at each church, multiple generations linked arms and worked together, with the younger learning from the older and the older being patient with the younger as they learn and understand. The age gap was not always easy to integrate on a mission trip or ministry team. Vacation Bible School (VBS) displays the various generations coming together around a shared vision and mission and linking arms to achieve the work together. As the church moves forward, the struggle is engaging the younger generations that have varied philosophies about church and ministry.

---

[2] Shaw, 147.

# Intergenerational Considerations

If you have been in an intergenerational environment, then you understand the facial expressions of various ages and preferred methods of communication that different ages utilize. You know the body language, how they spend time with one another, and how they interact with family. Since the church mirrors many aspects of an extended family, these same intergenerational factors appear with communication, preferences on how to spend time together, and other interpersonal expectations. Each leader must be aware of how people interact and prefer to receive and give information. In communication, these differences can bring people together or push them away.

The eleven other considerations include dress code, decision-making, meetings, policies, training, respect, loyalty, fun at work, knowledge transfer, feedback, and work ethic.[3] When you read about them, it becomes apparent that various generations approach these differently. You could have your grandparents' work ethic but differ on having fun at work. Generations can agree on the purpose of meetings or how to make decisions because they have done well transferring the knowledge over the years. Still, much time can be spent on these areas utilizing experiences and stories of how these various aspects were nuanced by a region, congregation, or family of origin. A community can have a history of being problematic and struggling to agree or understand one another.

Tim Elmore explains that one issue for younger adults in the workplace is that for the first time they spend the majority of their time with older adults rather than peers each day.[4] As this reality is the new normal, generational and age diversity can be leveraged as a strength. To create a "Gentelligent" workplace, there needs to be positive age climates and cultures that develop intergenerational social capital: "Four major roadblocks that prevent the development of Gentelligence: generational shaming, age biases, value perceptions, and knowledge differences."[5] This new area of generational diversity can be applied within the church to improve intergenerational relationships. Gentelligence is achieved when two goals have been met. First,

---

[3] Shaw, 7.

[4] Tim Elmore, *A New Kind of Diversity* (Duluth, GA: Maxwell Leadership, 2022), 181.

[5] Megan Gerhardt, Josephine Nachemson-Ekwall, and Brandon Fogel, *Gentelligence: The Revolutionary Approach to Leading an Intergenerational Workforce* (New York: Rowan and Littlefield, 2021), 45.

in an organization, generational tension and bias need to be broken down. Second, the organization must increase or build up its capacity to leverage intergenerational strength and power. Gentelligence is thus achieved through four practices. The first is to resist assumptions by breaking down the misunderstandings between generations.[6] The second practice is realized when the different generations can adjust their lens to see and understand the actions and behaviors of colleagues from other generations.[7] The third practice is to strengthen trust, which will require the different generations to change from adversaries to trusted, dependable partners.[8] The fourth is to "expand the pie" or negotiate and find a win-win solution from what appeared to be a win-lose scenario. The generations then stop competing and begin collaborating, thus creating more pie for everyone.[9] These four practices could refresh your people's understanding of each other and help them work together to the extent that the church synergy impacts the kingdom. As you think about the generational differences referenced by Shaw and Elmore, think about your church and the gap that exists among the different generations. How can you increase the Gentelligence within your church?

Mentoring relationships are one way to bring adults of various ages together. Coaching or career counseling is utilized in the business world to help make people's career goals more attainable. Older generations were taught how to do a job by being an apprentice or by learning from another employee on how to work within the established standards of the employer. Those in rural environments learned how to contribute to work on the family farm, usually by following in their parents' footsteps. As we encounter the early church in the New Testament, a model of entrusting or passing on knowledge, doctrine, effective ministry practices, and ways to live for Christ was passed through mentoring relationships and master/teacher relationships.

## Interprofessional Ministry

A practice primarily found in the medical field is known as interprofessional. This collaboration occurs when a team of people from two or

---

[6]  Gerhardt, Nachemson-Ekwall, and Fogel, 65.
[7]  Gerhardt, Nachemson-Ekwall, and Fogel, 70.
[8]  Gerhardt, Nachemson-Ekwall, and Fogel, 77.
[9]  Gerhardt, Nachemson-Ekwall, and Fogel, 82.

more different professions is willing to learn from one another to have effective collaboration with the goal that together, they can improve health outcomes. This team usually has nurses, physicians, social workers, psychologists, pharmacists, and therapists to address different aspects of care.[10] In the church, creating similar interprofessional mentoring groups across ages and areas of ministry focus would be a great approach to bringing generations together. The concept of bridging the generations for mutual understanding while also bringing various experiences and ministries together would increase discipleship and knowledge. The church could model this method even better than the medical community. This practice may seem unconventional for a ministry approach to the generations and ministry development, but it has the potential to enhance the overall work of making disciples.

One of the challenges that older generations struggle to grasp is how their life choices have impacted younger generations. Some evidence of this struggle can be found in relationships, finances, and careers that have caused the younger generations to delay adult practices. These young adults do not want the struggles they observed as kids. In addition, modern culture has created an anxiousness toward safety. Risk management was a business practice that transferred to child-rearing for Gen Xers and Millennials as their Boomer parents became aware of crimes against children.[11] You may remember seeing missing children milk cartons in school cafeterias. Each day, a child saw that they could be kidnapped. The perceived challenges created "anxiety over 'stranger danger'," that stemmed from "a displacement of other anxieties about the shifting understanding of family, of the increase of working mothers, of a weakening of community and the cohesion that accompanied it."[12] Generational challenges exist because younger generations desire to avoid the observed struggles of their parents and other adults of influence in their lives.

Adaptation in the church is different based on age, family of origin, and life experiences. People react to various emerging trends, morphing into new styles or rediscovering an old trend and learning

---

[10] "FAQ: What is an 'Interprofessional Team,' as Described in the Engages Teams Criterion," Accreditation Council for Continuing Medical Education, last modified February 5, 2021, https://www.accme.org/faq/what-interprofessional-team-described-engages-teams-criterion.

[11] Anne Helen Petersen, *Can't Even: How Millennials Became the Burnout Generation* (New York: Mariner, 2021), 30.

[12] Petersen, 31.

new models for doing life differently. Senior adults in your church were hesitant to have a phone installed in their house, followed by a bag phone in their car, a flip phone, and then a smartphone. This progression shows adaptations to emerging trends that resulted in morphing to a new style or option, ultimately leading to adults learning a new phone model multiple times over, with more recent editions and options being released. The same adaptation hesitation and processes exist within congregations as generations must consider adapting church schedules, new programs for ministry, and models that reimagine the local church.

## Generational Acceptance and Understanding

The need to change is observed throughout God's creation due to various factors. We adapt our clothing choices based on the weather. We must adjust each day to multiple factors that confront us. We change as conditions change, causing us to pivot to accomplish our to-do list. Adopting new ideas or models is different because it requires the individual to accept a new reality as their own. They adapt to a new community and tradition from the former place with other traditions and customs. We observe this best when we encounter another family and how they approach birthdays, holidays, and times when they gather. Every family opens presents differently or follows unique holiday traditions. Not every family eats and then opens presents at their grandparent's house on Christmas. Adapting to a new family through marriage and then embracing their traditions, although different from yours, takes a willingness to embrace how your spouse experienced life. In a local congregation, as new people come into the church and people age within the church, they constantly need to be adopted into the community. We learn from them, and they learn from the people in the church and together adapt and adopt to be the people God is calling his church to be in that community at that time. This ongoing process of change means the different generations can grow weary, lonely, or disenfranchised due to the various seasons of life. The opposite also can happen with people being excited, embraced, and connected to the congregation in a way that propels them forward.

Imagine your congregation gathered in worship. How many faces are in each generation? If you considered the oldest generation, how many people will likely not be a part of the congregation during the next decade? Do the numbers of younger faces emerging into adults balance the older generation? If they do, then your church has the capacity to continue into the future. Taking a snapshot view of the church is helpful to determine the balance of generations you are working with and how that impacts the years ahead. Socioeconomics is the next factor you need to understand among the generations. You may be surprised that the younger generation may give as much as the oldest generation in your church. The broad middle is the sweet spot for many churches because it is the largest block of giving units during their prime income-generating years and thus provides a considerable portion of the budget. This is not the case for every church, so the organization needs someone that can help chart the state of your finances among the generations. The church needs to understand the giving composite and how age can impact the overall health of the congregation. Diversity in age and finances are two factors among the generations that are healthy to understand. The last area of diversity is ethnic composition among the generations in the church. As communities become more diverse, the church should reflect a multiethnic picture of the region. Younger generations seem more open to this diversity than in past generations. You can drive through communities and see the diversity but then attend a local church, and the same reality is not true in the congregation.

## A Few Words of Caution for Your Reflection

Intergenerational differences are often viewed as a negative factor within the church. Instead, they can be one of the greatest strengths of a church that has one generation of disciples to mentor and entrust the faith to another generation of disciples. Often this can be an older person mentoring a younger person; however, this is not always the case. One of the first people I got to baptize in ministry was my grandmother, with her wheelchair and all. A disciple may not be older in age, but often the younger can learn much from the older people around them, and the older can learn from the younger. Challenges exist between age gaps or even people of a similar age, so take the time to bring generations together as they serve together in your congregation.

### Questions to Consider

1. What obstacle do you face in bringing the generations together to serve the church?

2. What are some tweaks that you could make to encourage those serving to develop relationships so they can pass on their experience and passion for ministry?

3. What does a snapshot of your congregation look like when you gather for worship? What are the different generations represented?

# PART 3:

# ORGANIZATIONAL COACHING

M any people need to be equipped within the organization to serve in a way that contributes to the mission. In college sports, the transfer portal is loved by some but troublesome for others. Organizations that recruited, invested, and then sees the talent move to another organization are often frustrated. In ministry, the transfer portal of people moving to another church with as little as a conversation, phone call, or social media message cuts deeper. Staff and volunteers often take a transfer portal approach to their involvement in church. Coaching is essential to recruit, invest, and equip talent within the organization. A coach is instrumental in developing a team mindset among teammates. Other leaders subdivide the group into parts to be further cultivated, but in the end, players will often recognize their coach as the one who invested in them. In church, we hear how much people appreciate the mentors that invested in their life, but most of the time, they state various people, including "my pastor." The following chapters seek to help all those mentors that invest in others to understand how to cultivate a team mindset in the organization, the challenges of a shrinking workforce in the church, the vitality metrics for performance accountability, and the need to streamline work to the simplest mean possible to achieve the vision and mission of the local church.

The book's last chapter highlights the challenge of a church transfer portal. Personal development and devotion encompass all the organizational challenges because a lack of walking with Christ causes people to struggle. If you are in the Word, praying, and focused on serving the people in the church, then it is hard to enter the transfer portal. Sometimes an event or situation causes people to need to move to a different church. Most of the struggle is related to a personal aspect of devotion to the Lord or spiritual immaturity that causes the transfer portal to even be considered. After all the investment and cultivation, the people of the church should reflect a more profound commitment than people of the lost world. As you read this section, reflect on your coaching and mentoring and consider those you cultivate through your influence and ministry.

## Chapter 11:

# Developing a Team Mindset

O ver the years, the phrase there is no "I" in team has become a popular statement in staff meetings. We all probably understand the underlying philosophy that, as a group, people work together for the best collective outcome for the team. Each person has a calling to contribute to the overall work of the church. As a part of the organization, people accomplish the mission and ministry as a collective body. I resonate with the "Working Genius" model developed by Patrick Lencioni because of the two foundational truths that he utilized. First, "people who utilize their natural, God-given talents are much more fulfilled and successful than those who don't."[1] We can agree that this is a desire and understanding that is not debated but embraced each week as the laypeople and ministers invest their talents in the local church. The second truth is that "teams and organizations that help people tap into their God-given talents are much more successful and productive than those that don't."[2] In the church, staff and volunteers are part of the team framework throughout the various ministries and administrative areas. Tidwell includes a third area, "total membership,"

---

[1] Patrick Lencioni, *The 6 Types of Working Genius* (Dallas: Matt Holt, 2022), 1.
[2] Lencioni, 1.

which includes everyone in the church who is a member. However, the church's work will involve many people serving through various roles and ministry groups. The leaders, whether volunteer or staff, must begin with esteem for all members.[3] To develop a team approach for ministry, the people of the church must remain the focus of each team.

In *The Secret Society of Success,* Tim Schurrer points out that many adults under fifty were trained to focus on their drive for success at all costs. In sports, academics, and career pursuits, individuals place themselves in the best position to succeed with the proper resumé, degree, and prospects for the job. They work hard to receive recognition and their next promotion.[4] This is a challenge in the church as people must shift from a self-promotion mindset to one of teamwork and service for the benefit of others. Everyone struggles as they hear the worldly message each day that to succeed they should focus on themselves and those they care about. Parents focus on the right schools and extracurricular activities to get their children into the best colleges. Adults are focused on the next status symbol or at least maintaining the status they have obtained. This infiltrates the church, as some people think being a leader, whether elder, deacon, Bible teacher, team leader, or committee chairperson, will improve their influence and status. Jesus challenged the disciples against this mindset. Among those disciples closest to him who began to ask who would be granted the seats to his left and right, Jesus rebuked them for having a misguided perspective of his ministry. They were challenged to model servanthood and the sacrifice of humility, as seen in Luke 9.

Everyone enjoys appreciation. Most team members need help understanding the pressure and stresses they may encounter and the weight of those concerns as a volunteer or paid worker. Most people in ministry play a supporting role on the team. Your organization will likely never have a staff meeting where people think they have too much help. Team leaders often think they are doing a great job of appreciating their team, but some people confuse appreciation with cheerleading. In the sport of cheering on others, the goal is to increase team spirit and get everyone engaged and excited, which can be encouraging. Appreciation lets team members know they are valued and they fulfill an essential need on the team. The Bible provides us with

---

[3] Tidwell, *Church Administration,* 137 (see chap.1, n.5).

[4] Tim Schurrer, *The Secret Society of Success* (Nashville: Nelson, 2022), 45.

many leaders who did not know how to value the people they relied on to accomplish the work.

In Exodus, Pharaoh did not value team in his hierarchal system of government in Egypt. Moses continuously came to him with words from the Lord promising plagues if Pharaoh did not let the people go. Pharaoh witnessed a progression of destruction from the Lord, but he would not relent. He would make promises and then not follow through. This created mistrust and confusion among the people as they lost livelihood, family, and food, leading to destitution. Fast forward to today, the circumstances on our ministry teams are different, but if they are led by dictators and the team leader does not follow through with commitments, mistrust and confusion will follow. You may not experience plagues, but you may suffer many challenges before the team leader relents and surrenders to team consensus. Leadership plagues are brutal in the church as staff and volunteers resign, programs do not align with mission, and people cannot get the answers they need. No leader desires to cultivate or model this culture; nevertheless, accountability for leaders to prevent "Pharoah" leadership is often missing in the local church. Western styles of leadership often create leaders who are unwilling to be humble.

Patrick Lencioni outlines five dysfunctions for teams that apply in business and the church. The first dysfunction stems from team members' unwillingness to be vulnerable with each other, revealing an absence of trust. If a team lacks trust, their second dysfunction will be fear of conflict, as they hesitate to debate ideas and settle for veiled discussions and guarded comments. The lack of conflict leads to the third dysfunction of lack of investment in the work because opinions and debates were discouraged, causing low commitment levels. Lack of accountability is the fourth dysfunction. The team has yet to buy in, and their lack of commitment leads to avoiding accountability in their work. Team members do not engage others to improve or correct behaviors that work against the betterment of the team. When this happens, the environment fosters inattentiveness to results. This results in the fifth dysfunction of an individualistic approach where ego, career advancement, promotion, or the need for personal recognition causes friction on the team which leads to inattention to results.[5]

---

[5] Patrick Lencioni, *The Five Dysfunctions of a Team* (San Francisco, CA: Jossey-Bass, 2002), 189.

These dysfunctions can wreak havoc in a church or ministry team. Developing those serving in ministry to have a healthy approach to the collaborative work of ministry is essential.

A research study conducted with more than 250 church leadership teams over two years identified five disciplines of thriving teams: focusing on purpose, leveraging differences within team membership, leading through inspiration rather than control, structuring intentional decision making, and building a culture of continuous collaboration.[6] Developing a team mindset among staff and volunteers can be a challenge due to the size of the organization, historical leadership mistakes, or prescribed formalities. These five disciplines are not overly complicated but require staff and volunteers to understand and be willing to employ them within the team. Take a moment to imagine how these disciplines are already in use or lacking within your team.

As you consider the people in your ministry and the desire to cultivate a team culture, take some time and pray for the people on your team(s). People are often looking for an exit ramp because they are not being utilized in a way that makes them feel they are adding value to the kingdom. Elmore states it this way:

> Every challenge we encounter is either a problem to solve or a tension to manage. Tension, however, is a normal part of leading a team of people. We will never rid ourselves of certain tensions; they are to be managed and not expected to disappear. However, different people from different generations who join our team come with problems that need to be solved or, better yet, prevented.[7]

As churches gain volunteers and staff members, we must remind ourselves that they bring many great traits to the team as well as problems that need to be solved.

Growing up, I worked on many projects with my grandfather. Sometimes I knew a quicker or easier way to complete something, but a new idea or opinion was not invited. I served only as the extra set of hands needed. This often created tension between us as we strived to work together. Have you ever inherited a prescribed way of completing a task? Maybe you have been a leader and hired a staff member

---

[6]  Ryan T. Hartwig and Warren Bird, *Teams That Thrive: Five Disciplines of Collaborative Leadership* (Downers Grove, IL: IVP, 2015), 86.

[7]  Elmore, *A New Kind of Diversity,* 168 (see chap.10, n.3).

of a different generation that did not follow your plan. They were younger, and you did not approach the work from the same perspective, or maybe they were older and did not receive good supervision from someone younger. As people move from another local church to join a different church, it is vital to understand the problems that have been left unsolved and what can be prevented. Eventually, issues will resurface if they have not been considered and resolved. This also can be true of staff that left another position to join your team, as they may not have resolved the issues that caused them to consider moving to another place.

It is always helpful to consider the size of your organization. Hartwig and Bird provide this perspective:

> In smaller churches the teams are typically made of mostly volunteers plus a pastor or other staff such as the pastor's administrative assistant. As a church increases in size, the senior leadership team often draws only from staff members. In even larger churches, it's typically certain members of the executive staff…You need an outstanding team because it sets the pace for almost everything in the life of your church. For good or bad, leadership teams shape the culture, direct the mission, establish the vision and model the values of your church.[8]

As you consider the size of your church, Hartwig and Bird's perspective can help you understand the congregation's relationship to leadership. In a smaller church with laity involved in the day-to-day decision-making, it is critical to understand the influencers of the team. The administrative assistant, for instance, can have more influence than most and can influence each aspect of the church and the people.

As you understand your ministry setting and identify the team members, you can begin to invest in them with the vision that guides every decision. Values are entrusted to others as you model those, and they flow through the team to other faithful leaders as the culture is shaped through those values. The group begins to direct the mission the leadership is moving the church to embrace. This level of synergy for leadership is called organizational management credibility that can only occur as team members embrace the direction of the team leader.

---

[8] Hartwig and Bird, *Teams That Thrive*, 32–33.

Various challenges will arise as a team moves together, and one of those can be generational differences toward the church.

## People Challenges with a Team Mindset

The difference between generations and how we approach our work leads to different expectations, evidenced by age and the inherited values in approaches to church. A few challenges that are worthy of discussion found in the book *A New Kind of Diversity* include mental health issues such as anxiety, depression, and high stress experienced by adults. Diverse generations embrace various mindsets, such as the "free agent" mindset, that can be a challenge within your team. As the name suggests, a "free agent" is not committed to the organization. Another challenge is the range in personalities, strengths, and leadership styles that can create trials for a team. Additionally, each organization will have to navigate the challenges that technology has created by lowering emotional intelligence.[9]

Difficult situations or conflict can cause people to look for the next exit ramp available to leave the ministry. As I encounter a difficult situation, I conduct a quick assessment. Does this issue involve people, property, programs, or more than one of these areas? If the problem is with people, my next step is to determine if it is isolated or recurring. Each issue with people will be nuanced, but the first step should be meeting with the people to understand the problem firsthand. Teams cannot function if the conflict continues unresolved among team members. As servant leaders, the people's posture should continually be to live at peace as we work together. If the issue is property related, it will impact the team by causing frustrations, but it is usually easier for the leader to address. Many times, the difficulties with property can be shared spaces between leaders and ministries or scheduling of space for specific ministries or leaders. Sometimes people get the impression a ministry team controls a space, should be favored over others in event or location assignments, or owns resources, which causes struggles with other teams. We discussed in chapter two the complete picture of administering a property. Still, one more aspect for every ministry team is working well with those that set up and clean, so the team does not get the reputation of not caring for the

---

[9]  Elmore, *A New Kind of Diversity,* 175.

facility or being difficult to work with. Another trigger for the team could be programming-related struggles with the church's structure or the previous way a leader directed the mission and vision of the church. Some team members will bring ideas from other churches or ministries their friends attend. These program ideas can cause issues when presented negatively rather than from a desire to see the ministry flourish. The enemy can use any of the three areas to cause team members to compare, have conflict, or lack unity. Placing people on teams based on their giftedness and ability to contribute to the overall work in a healthy way will greatly reduce issues.

Getting people to think beyond what makes their life easier will enhance team development. As people feel overwhelmed, the only thing that seems possible is completing the task at hand. A leader's challenge is to help everyone understand what can only be accomplished if a team moves together in the same direction. If team members attempt their work alone, the organization suffers because the overall ministry impact is diminished. According to Emily Dean, "In leadership you will need to build a support system both inside and outside of the ministry you serve. As you develop leaders to serve alongside you, you will be creating much-needed support and connections. Being friends with those you serve is healthy."[10] Ministry teams are interconnected and should be one of the most significant places of support and opportunities for growth. Unfortunately, this is not the experience of everyone that serves in ministry through the local church. Nurturing members and helping them overcome any bad experiences is a needed focus for ministry leaders.

Social mobility usually speaks to upward trajectories where someone improves their standing in society by increasing in wealth and class. The opposite can also be true in a society with a downward trajectory where someone loses status by moving downward in the social class system. As you ponder people's upward, horizontal, and downward options and how they relate to the interconnectedness of team members, consider that ministry can have the same three options. The team can help improve the work, become stagnant, or cause the church to decline. Team members should evaluate whether they are making contributions toward an upward kingdom impact, horizontal complacency, or a downward trajectory. Each church has a constant

---

[10] Emily Dean, *Women Leading Well: Stewarding the Gift of Ministry Leadership* (Brentwood, TN: B&H Academic, 2023), 111.

churn of leaving. Even leaders that teach, deacons that serve, or staff on the team find other opportunities, burn out, or decide to move on without notice. Each church has a culture and people may eventually feel they no longer fit within the framework. Team leaders must be trained to invest in the team because together, the people will define the culture as they execute their work unto Christ and his church.

## Understanding a Team Mindset

Have you ever been on a dysfunctional team? Think about a time when you had to be in a group at school and work together on an assignment. Some people have horrible experiences from bullying or doing all the work on every group project because others did not pull their weight on a team. These same struggles and mindsets also creep into the church through committees, supervisory structures, and workgroups. Sometimes previous negative experiences affect our attitudes towards teams. Team members must understand one another. Finding time to cultivate relationships beyond working together will grow a stronger team. You do not have to find a retreat setting, a ropes course outing, or sit in a circle and share your feelings, but you do need to know each other well enough to relate to one another. While team exercises can be beneficial, there are many ways to build relationships. This can be challenging for some leaders, especially men, to break the barriers to gain understanding. Still, team success is dependent upon understanding one another to the level of mutual respect for the person and their place on the team. T. J. Addington provides an excellent description of how a church team should be defined:

> Many people have a faulty understanding of what it means to serve on a team. This includes thinking that teams are about working with our buddies, getting our emotional needs met, doing life with our close friends, spending lots of time together, attending meetings, or working on the same project. Or, that because we are a team, we lead by committee. No! A high-impact team is a group of missionally aligned and healthy individuals working strategically together under good leadership toward common objectives, with accountability for results.[11]

---

[11] T. J. Addington, *Leading from the Sandbox* (Colorado Springs: NavPress, 2010), 17.

Most ministers would tell you they desire to see their ministry teams make an impact and work together well. People that agree together on the mission have a shared philosophy, are healthy in all aspects of life, have a good leader for the team to achieve agreed-upon objectives, and have accountability for outcomes.

Leadership styles, life experiences, and communication are contributing factors to being able to function effectively on a team. The cohesion will increase as these are learned through assessments and working together on the team. If your team rotates consistently with team members, having cohesion can be a challenge. The generational differences discussed earlier should be considered in work because of how they approach working with others, sharing their ideas, and collaborating with the team.

The progression of developing a team culture entered American culture in the 1960s. By the 1990s, people projected growth in business through utilizing teams as a means to enhance the work of the organization. You see this progression in the church as the dynamics have moved from departments and structures of hierarchy to a more engaged collaborative effort. Views of teams have changed over time; but typically, having an odd number of people helps a team navigate challenges and conflict. Many stories could be shared of the dysfunctions of groups of people in the church; however, more memories exist of seeing a team gel and become more like family than team members. A mission trip where senior adults link arms with teenagers and build houses is just one example. Process-driven meetings evolve into a brainstorming family that openly shares their opinions to create tension that moves everyone forward. The years of VBS would not have happened had some devoted volunteers not worked countless hours together to plan and pray. These stories provide a mental image of McMillan's rationale that the essential ingredient in team success is a clear, common, and compelling task to accomplish together.[12]

According to Elmore, "If we care about the future, we must care about connecting with and equipping the generations behind us to lead well."[13]

## Questions to Consider

These considerations are riveting when we pause and consider that when people on a team do not feel valued, then over time, the passion

---

[12] Pat MacMillan, *The Performance Factor* (Nashville: B&H, 2001), 35.
[13] Elmore, *A New Kind of Diversity*, 42.

for their work erodes, and even burnout occurs. When these two things begin to happen, most people begin looking for a new opportunity, or Schurrer states they begin looking for what's next.[14]

### Questions to Consider

1. How could you improve the way you express appreciation to your team?
2. Do you tend only to deal with people when an issue or problem arises due to your time constraints?
3. Do the people on your team feel valued?
4. What support systems are in place for team members as they serve?

---

[14] Schurrer, *The Secret Society of Success*, 43.

## Chapter 12:

# Shrinking Workforce

M eet Sarah, a young college student who loves to serve and is willing to help the church, but she has been offered double the money at a local business. The struggle with young adults is that church salaries often do not keep up with inflation. Some can afford to take a small paying job at the church, but for many, living costs are more than a person can manage. Nathan loves students and families and serves his current church well, but with a growing family, he has begun the search for better pay in a more stable church environment. The people love Nathan but have yet to learn he is on food stamps due to his ministerial pay. Kevin has pastored for years at the same church. He has raised his family and loved the congregation, but he is in his late fifties and wondering if he should do something else until he retires. Leslie is a gifted leader, but she does not feel she can continue to serve in the local church because the pastor's demands to grow the congregation and the helicopter parenting and risk factors of children's ministry have become more than she can handle. She has started looking at para-church organizations for a shift from children's ministry. This chapter examines a few reasons and societal shifts that are leading to fewer people considering church staff and volunteer positions.

Have you heard anyone express having burnout, anxious thoughts, feelings of being hurried, or even weariness in their work or personal life? A simple definition of being weary is being "very tired, especially after you have been working hard or doing something for a long time."[1] In the months following the lingering impacts of having COVID-19, I became weary and burdened. I did not desire to be weary or tired all the time, but my body was feeling excessive exertion from sickness and the longer-than-expected season of recovery. In my lifetime, this is the first time as a population we seem to be experiencing this level of collective weariness for months at a time. We had some signs of weariness during 9/11 when the United States was attacked. We watched on television as the Twin Towers came down and thousands perished. Accounts of people during World War II reveal how our nation endured weariness. Societal crises during the Great Depression or the Flu Pandemic of 1918 are just a few examples over the past century. We see many periods in history where challenges in the world, natural disasters, or regional events seem to bring a collective weariness to the people. The Bible reveals countless stories of times when people had collective pressures or worries that caused them to seem hopeless, alone, or desiring a former existence. The people following Moses in the wilderness had a range of collective emotions from their plight.

Consider Jesus with his disciples and their range of questions and expectations of being a part of his kingdom. He gave us words of encouragement about an unresponsive generation in Matt 11:28: "Come to me, all of you who are weary and burdened, and I will give you rest." Many people are not prepared mentally, emotionally, spiritually, or physically to deal with an ongoing period of crisis.

People have had to navigate challenging times throughout history. With all the modern conveniences, it is hard to imagine that today is more complicated than at any other time. Still, the difficulty is different. Digital interaction and advancements are quick and life changing. However, many young adults have always been digitally connected with the ability to interact with a non-human for automated answers and solutions. Artificial Intelligence (AI) is changing how people interact with challenges. Its negative effects include struggling with

---

[1] *Oxford Learner's Dictionary*. "Weary (adj)," *https*://www.oxfordlearnersdictionaries.com /us/definition/english/weary.

privacy, personal safety, the absence of emotional intelligence, unfair or biased outcomes, or hindering societal advancement.[2] AI also creates challenges for the church, with a volunteer workforce being humans that serve in many areas of ministry. A shrinking workforce has not relegated the church to replace the human component of serving or loving our neighbors. Some aspects of human existence and how we care for and serve one another cannot be automated with technology.

Church attendance has wavered since the COVID-19 pandemic through programming, weekly ministry opportunities, and travel experiences that ebb and flow based on events in society and their personal lives. People struggle to get back to a rhythm of life with the workforce demands, family needs, and community outside the church, which has produced mixed opinions on whether churches will maintain a level of community experienced by previous generations. People can utilize a smart home, dictation software, and remote work platforms but still must engage their mind in the work to do it. You may not manually get up and change the thermostat, but you swipe to open an app or press a button for the temperature to change. This new reality for the church to navigate may provide fewer options for a workforce but more resources to accomplish tasks, creating a frustrating combination.

The COVID-19 pandemic created a few markers for people to evaluate their time and involvement. During the height of the pandemic, volunteers had less stress, fewer meetings, and reduced preparation time. A return to being as scheduled or busy as before caught many congregations off guard. Congregations desire the same level of programming, but the workforce has not been willing to engage at their previous commitment levels. Paid staff has also shrunk due to the stress load of ministry demands and workforce options that allow them to engage with lost people and make disciples through secular opportunities. Ministers are now looking at non-traditional paths to their calling. The Great Resignation has impacted ministers who are also considering leaving the ministry.[3]

It is normal in ministry to have staff turnover or times when staff members need to take sabbaticals. The struggle churches are facing

---

[2] Forbes Technology Council, "14 Ways AI Could Become a Detriment to Society," *Forbes,* June 14, 2021, https://www.forbes.com/sites/forbestechcouncil/2021/06/14/14-ways-ai-could-become-a-detriment-to-society/?sh=219e164527fe.

[3] Melissa Florer-Bixler, "Why Pastors are Joining the Great Resignation," *Sojourners,* November 30, 2021, *https://*sojo.net/articles/why-pastors-are-joining-great-resignation.

presently is a shrinking workforce. It is common today to hear of a church looking for a pastor or struggling to find associates for music, children, youth, or discipleship ministers. Dwindling volunteer bases are also prevalent in churches as life situations have people agreeing to serve for fixed ranges of time that are longer than a season or semester.[4]

## Factors for Shrinking Workforce

It may seem to some like ministry has more challenges today than when they first began. As these challenges have been expressed, fewer people step forward to serve. Some have found other ways to serve in their communities. For example, someone might become a chaplain for their child's travel ball team who can ensure the team watches a worship service online each weekend or has devotion time when traveling. For years children had parents involved locally in sports and art programs who were still faithful to church Sundays and Wednesdays. The schedule and cultural shifts may not pivot back, but the shrinking workforce is partly due to the shifting of the church schedule and ministries appearing to need less people. Each time the once-a-month attendee arrives, the doors are open, people are greeted, and the worship service is conducted. They do not see the challenges of the behind-the-scenes shrinking volunteer workforce.

If you ask a pastor if he likes his student or worship minister, his response will probably be that we are not looking to replace anyone. More focus has been placed in recent years on calling out the called.[5] This focus is simply the renewed effort to invite people to consider being in ministry as a pastor, missionary, or other minister. Think back to your first volunteer or paid position. Who asked you to serve or first planted the seed that they thought you had potential for ministry? Most of the time, someone mentioned it and asked you to pray about it. Although people are busy it does not mean people are not willing to serve if asked. People and schedules will always be a factor, but we still must be leaders who push against the dwindling workforce by doing our part to mentor, invite, and cast a vision for ministry.

---

[4] Carey Nieuwhof, "10 Reasons Church Attendance is Declining (Even for Committed Christians)," *Carey Nieuwhof (blog)*, https://careynieuwhof.com/10-reasons-even-committed-church-attenders-attending-less-often/.

[5] Scott Pace and Shane Pruitt, *Calling Out the Called* (Nashville: B&H, 2022).

In every business you enter, whether you are eating, buying a television, or getting milk, you usually see a hiring sign. This seems to be a common theme for businesses as well as churches as they try to fill vacancies. News outlets have been asking where the younger workers are or what we will do as a society when the older adults stop working. The church is asking the same questions as they seek to add staff members or find volunteers. Your church may be in a place where you are fully staffed and have a healthy pipeline of volunteers, but many churches are wondering how to staff everything in the new reality. A shrinking workforce from staff to volunteers strains most of the church's current programming models. Inflation causes price increases for businesses as they try to keep pace with rising costs. A full-time employee at Hobby Lobby can make more than $18 per hour, and Target pays up to $24 per hour for full-time work.[6] The yearly compensation for Hobby Lobby would be $38,480 plus benefits,[7] while Target employees make $49,920 plus benefits. These two retail jobs demonstrate the challenge that many in support or ministerial staff roles can make more to care for their families by working at a business and not the church. This challenge is not shrinking the workforce as much as it is straining the workforce. Bi-vocational ministers have been on the rise as these challenges are impacting the churches.[8] The low pay as an intern or introductory position of church staff is appealing to missionally-minded emerging adults until they must balance their monthly expenses against their church or para-church ministry stipend.

A shrinking workforce is hard to manage when fewer people are available for positions. The church has fewer options in their search, and the minister has more choices as they seek where they should serve. Carey Nieuwhof provides a perspective on hiring new team

---

[6] Target Corporation, "Target to Set New Starting Wage Range and Expand Access to Health Care Benefits to More Team Members," *A Bullseye View,* February 28, 2022, https://corporate.target.com/press/releases/2022/02/target-to-set-new-starting-wage-range-and-expand-a.

[7] Ashley Wilemon, "Hobby Lobby Raises Minimum Wage to $18.50," *Hobby Lobby Newsroom,* December 14, 2021, https://newsroom.hobbylobby.com/articles/hobby-lobby-raises-minimum-wage-to-18-50.

[8] Thom S. Rainer, "The Bi-vocational Revolution Most Churches are Missing," *Church Answers (blog),* October 4, 2021, https://churchanswers.com/blog/the-bi-vocational-revolution-most-churches-are-missing/#:~:text=And%20it%20is%20a%20movement%20that%20has%20accelerated%20the%20past%20two%20years.&text=Though%20we%20don't%20have,one%20bi%2Dvocational%20staff%20member.

members in light of five future staffing trends in the post Great Resignation age.[9] Consider these five trends in light of paid and volunteer team members. First, "Your future staff expect you to work for them," and as a result, "if you help them win, you'll both win. If you merely want them to help you win, you'll lose."[10] Second, your staff will show diminished loyalty because they know there are many options if the job does not work out. Third, a healthy church culture will be attractive, whereas an anemic or toxic church will cause people to consider leaving. Compensation is not enough for a person if they are miserable. The younger generation is willing to work if passion is evident. The fourth is a positive trend because as the younger workforce does not work in mediocre organizations, they are attracted to "talent density."[11] The church may have to think about fewer people in their workforce but have better, more effective staff. If you can create an effective team, it will naturally attract more people. If you have been around the church or business for a few years, you may have experienced an open position that required several people to replace the former staff member when they left. This refers to "talent density" in that the right gifted people in a position usually get more accomplished. Millennials and younger generations are fueled by being part of something meaningful and fulfilling the greater good. The fifth and last trend is that "young leaders will show up ready to fuel your mission."[12] If your organization cannot articulate its mission, then you will struggle to attract or keep younger workers. They are not impressed with "leaders who want to preserve the institution, pad the bottom line, or simply grow the organization will always struggle to attract and keep young leaders."[13]

---

[9] The Great Resignation is what occurred during the COVID-19 pandemic as people voluntarily resigned from their employment post-pandemic for various reasons.

[10] Carey Nieuwhof, "How to Hire for the Future: 5 Future Staffing Trends to Watch as You Recruit Your New Team Members," *Carey Nieuwhof (blog)*, https://careynieuwhof.com /how-to-hire-for-the-future-5-future-staffing-trends-to-watch-as-you-recruit-your-new-team -members/?he=jdean%40nobts.edu&el=email&utm_source=ActiveCampaign&utm_medium =email&utm_content=Why+is+it+so+hard+to+hire+%28and+keep%29+great+people %3F&utm_campaign=4%2F22+-+How+to+Hire+for+the+Future.

[11] Nieuwhof, "How to Hire for the Future."

[12] Nieuwhof, "How to Hire for the Future."

[13] Nieuwhof, "How to Hire for the Future."

# Navigating Adults' Expectations for Ministry

As the focus shifts in ministries in the church, the workforce can be slower to pivot to staffing those areas. Discipleship, family ministry, and worship are three areas that are spoken of more today. Some estimate that 20 percent of Southern Baptist churches are searching for their next lead pastor. As the need grows, and more vacancies are realized, another factor for the church is that the minister expects more from the organization. Younger adults desire to be coached and mentored for their life of service to the Lord. Emerging adults' lives have been provided with educational and development opportunities for each challenge of their journeys. Opportunities to further their education, attend conferences, or find a network of relationships to nurture their growth are normal for them. This expectation is one that larger churches have more accessibility to provide both internally and through outside connections to other networks.

Coaching can be undervalued in smaller organizations because the expectation is to execute the position's duties. In a smaller church, older members are prepared to explain or direct the areas of business, so they undervalue the ministerial coaching that can help emerging adults succeed on staff. My first staff position for children and youth at age eighteen included direction to execute my duties rather than holistic coaching for ministry. This was a church that had a history of churning through ministers for various reasons, which led younger generations that observed the church's struggles to be open to non-church staff positions in ministry. I am thankful for several mentors, including my home church pastor, campus minister, and longtime friend in ministry. These men helped guide me through the struggles and challenges of serving on staff.

Unclear expectations on ministerial care and treatment of the staff has driven many to parachurch ministries. If you are a layperson, ponder and pray through how you could care for ministers in your church. Think about how you have treated the staff over the years in the church. As a minister, examine your experiences and determine how you could coach others, maybe even on another church staff. As many are struggling, think about ways to help network and coach others in ministry. You may find yourself struggling. It is okay to reach out to someone for help before it is too late.

Having diminishing options is not ideal in any business area. A shrinking pool means fewer options, with quality being one factor people desire when considering filling a vacancy on their team. Fewer options translate into some churches becoming more desperate and thus lessening their threshold for staff. However, the process for vetting staff for a volunteer or paid position should be a maintained standard of identifying the best candidate for a vacancy. The church should strive for more than simply asking, "Is anyone available?"

## Developing the Younger Generation

One way to help the church is to involve the younger generation as soon as possible in the church's ministries. Children and students can serve in many ways in the church as minors. They can be a part of first impressions or serve in different ministries with their families and begin to be grafted into the church as they mature into adulthood. This is a great way to expand the workforce by allowing the younger generations of the church not to wait to begin in ministry but to become regular servants in the church. As young people become a part of the serving team through church ministries, a connection is established beyond attending that propels them to love the church. Internships or volunteer programs have helped school-age children, especially teens, have opportunities to experience some staff responsibilities.

Larger churches are solving the shrinking workforce by finding people with potential and mentoring them within the church to grow into leadership positions on staff. This solution does not solve the shrinking workforce for most churches since they are smaller and not always in a large community. Seminaries, state conventions, and associations have always been a resource to help ministers and churches find each other as vacancies occur. These places where churches have historically found potential candidates for their vacancies have fewer options to offer, and there are not enough ministers in these areas. More leaders are speaking to the issue of a shrinking workforce, emphasizing how to nurture ways to call people to respond to ministry through the church.

The chapter on generational differences and diversity within our ministry contexts revealed that we have more adults trying to mind the gap in their ages but fewer people feeling called to vocational ministry. Attendance shifts have caused the church to have fewer weekly volunteers. A recent study by Barna Group revealed that more pastors are unsure of a call to pastor their church. Stressors from the endless nonstop grind of ministry have caused problems for many leaders.

Forty-two percent of full-time pastors have considered quitting. The top three reasons that ministers considered quitting are the stress of work, feeling isolated and lonely, and political divisions.[14] The old statistic that 20 percent of the people do most of the work is something I remember from childhood, but today the number could even be less in some contexts. Due to changing life patterns, fears, and schedule conflicts, the shrinking workforce wants to know what options or solutions are available. In Southern Baptist life, an initiative was birthed by two SBC leaders to address this concern by focusing on "Calling out the Called."[15] People need a compelling *ask* to be willing to accept a position with ongoing time and commitment requirements. Volunteers can feel recruiting fatigue because it never ends. People within the organization can get numb to the generic requests of help. An intentional personal invitation allows a discussion of the need and how it fits each person's gifts, talents, and interests.

A person moving from attending a worship service to an ongoing responsibility is a more significant step for some people than ministry leaders realize. A call to vocational ministry, missionary to the nations, or an ongoing ministry volunteer can incite fear or hesitancy toward taking the steps, and those already serving may not realize how hard that leap of faith can be for the disciple.

The intern or nontraditional staffing structures that reflect corporate America's shift toward consulting, temp agencies for staffing, and value-driven talent recruitment for limited pay or no pay positions have impacted ministry positions as churches have considered ways to staff the ongoing needs with a smaller workforce. In the eighties and nineties, it was common for smaller to medium size churches to utilize college and seminary students for summer staff positions when ministry events and trips were more intense and relied on volunteers during the school year. As a seminary professor, I have seen more churches in recent years attempt to bring the ten-to-twelve-week summer staff member back to try a hybrid staffing approach and lessen the budget burden of permanent staff.

Some employers fill in the gaps by utilizing a temp agency, gaining a workforce that does not require vacation or benefits and avoiding payroll taxes because the temp agency invoices the employer for hours

---

[14] Barna Group, "Pastors Share Top Reasons They've Considered Quitting Ministry in the Past Year," *Barna,* April 27, 2022, https://www.barna.com/research/pastors-quitting-ministry/.

[15] Scott Pace and Shane Pruitt, *Calling Out the Called* (Nashville: B&H, 2022), 2.

worked. Options like this can provide a "template for the contemporary work model, in which adjuncts, independent contractors, freelancers, gig employees, or any other sort of 'contingent' laborer make up a new, ever-expanding societal classification: the precariat."[16] Churches utilize the precariat workforce through intern and residency programs to increase their staff capacity. On the other hand, the "salariat" or "the class of workers who are salaried, have agency within their jobs, and report feeling that their opinion counts within the company."[17] Often when full-time workers retire or are laid off, they are replaced with independent contractors or the precariat. As the workforce experiences this shift, churches are also exploring precariat and salariat workforce solutions. Churches are not alone in staffing challenges, but as in previous times of transition, should always make each staff search and decision a matter of prayer.

### Questions to Consider

1. The church should set an example of respecting people and their organizational contributions. A church should not utilize a person on staff to the extent they need two other jobs to make ends meet. Does your organization value and care for their people by providing for their needs?
2. How can your church not drift into a temp agency mindset for staff positions?
3. What resources can you provide for the ministerial staff to help them with stress, loneliness, and political divides?
4. Pick a minister and commit to calling, sending cards, and building a relationship to care for them.

---

[16] Petersen, *Can't Even,* 96 (see chap.10, n.10).
[17] Petersen, 98.

## Chapter 13:

# Personal Development and Devotion

I was recently having lunch at a restaurant when I noticed three older ladies talking about church and the Bible at the table next to mine. Their conversation was easy to overhear since the tables were close together and they were talking loudly. One lady stated that she thought she knew the Bible well after attending church all these years, including Sunday School. Her following statement was surprising: "As I was reading my Bible the other day, it dawned on me that I did not know the Bible as well as I thought I did after all these years of being in church and Bible study!" The other ladies chimed in with what they were learning, and at that point, our waitress arrived to take our order, and my attention moved on. This conversation reminds us that just because people are available, faithful, and attending does not mean they are progressively developing spiritually. The intentional development of staff, leaders, and volunteers is vital to ministry leadership. Each congregation depends on a development process that produces devoted disciples that desire to serve their local church.

Pastors, ministers, directors, volunteers, and missionaries are needed. It requires devoted disciples to serve faithfully each week so people can hear the gospel, respond, and then follow God's call to serve. As leaders in any capacity through the local church, reaching and making disciples remains a crucial component to leading and managing the organization. If helping people become more devoted disciples is not managed, many other aspects of life and work will need attention. As you address those, you need to be more engaged with the primary tasks in your personal life. People become so overwhelmed in managing their lives that walking with Christ is marginalized. This topic is needed in our ministry management plans more so than business processes. Take a moment and consider your previous few weeks. What development opportunities or action steps did you take to grow as a ministry leader? Did you engage in spiritual habits to be a more devoted disciple of Christ?

A ministers' associational meeting on a Monday may have several senior adult men chatting about the church and telling a younger pastor that resigning on mornings like these is tempting. A Monday morning following a long Sunday can be a challenge for volunteers or ministers who gave everything they had left and were still frazzled when they finished. Each week countless volunteers have felt that it was not enough or that their people were not engaged or cared for. You have probably witnessed this in many ministers, from children's volunteers to your church's adult small group leaders. Ministers often find themselves reconsidering their callings or pondering whether they should continue the work. When I was called to ministry and volunteered in high school, I remember some great moments in serving. I still have notes and journal thoughts from those years showing how the Lord continued to meet me where I was. Through the circumstances, and even when I thought it was not enough, God was moving among his people. My pastor was a faithful man who was giving his all through leadership struggles to keep a church moving in the right direction with the vision the Lord had revealed to him. I do not remember the sermon titles or the business meeting agendas, but I remember a man who faithfully preached each week and shared how the Lord worked in his life. He often spoke of his prayer partner that also provided personal accountability. His transparency was captivating, and his heart for the Lord was unwavering.

Commitment at all costs was modeled by the church staff throughout my childhood. The struggles, whether criticism, staff challenges, or growth requiring new space, were tackled and overcome. If you

desire to fulfill your calling faithfully, you must rise above the circumstances and struggles and continue to return to the Lord. In Isaiah
35, we see the people of God return to Zion. They were weary of their
rebellion and from turning away from God. The struggle had taken
a toll on the people: "Strengthen the weak hands, steady the shaking
knees! Say to the cowardly: Be strong; do not fear!"[1] These verses
indicate the people were exhausted, weak in their physical and emotional strength, and fearful during this time. In ministry, I believe the
people of God on staff or the church's volunteer staff each week can
feel the same, especially when their daily devotions and walks with
the Lord are wavering.

Spiritual habits should be evidenced among the people of God
but especially among the people that lead and teach each week. In a
click-or-swipe culture, from websites to apps, we must be diligent in
developing staff spiritually, not just training them in ministry execution with performance metrics. You may be asking how this is part of
the administrative work of the church. If we do not administer a plan
for growth and development in the spiritual components of ministry,
then our people will wander or rebel as the people did in the Scriptures
over time. People historically grow weary, discontented, or even have
rose-colored glasses when thinking about the past. Many Old Testament stories show the people of God being passionate but then growing tired, weary, bored, rebelling, and finally returning to God. As the
New Testament reveals the birth of the early church and the spiritual
leadership and interpersonal challenges they faced, we understand that
administering a plan for personal development and devotion should be
a priority in the ongoing administrative tasks of the leader. Does the
church office open with a devotion and prayer each day? Consider a
five-minute pause to pray on the job. What are the possibilities if the
custodians, office staff, or ministerial staff were nurtured spiritually?

We can become efficient with people, property, and finances
with the personal ability to make it happen each week. Managing the
organization in all these areas is vital to supporting the overall work
of the church, and they need daily attention. However, spiritual development is only sometimes considered. At times, it is not consistently detectable with the people we lead, whether a paid staff member
or volunteer serving. Over time, the lack of administering a personal

---

[1] Isa 35:3–4a.

and committed devotion to the Lord will become evident as the people need to develop their daily habits of walking with the Lord. Tod Bolsinger expresses it this way for ministry leaders:

> Leadership is energizing a community of people toward their transformation in order to accomplish a shared mission in the face of a changing world. Leadership (as differentiated from management or stewardship) is about transformation and mission, about growing and going, about personal development and corporate effectiveness—simultaneously. We know we are facing a leadership challenge if it requires us to grow as leaders and as people, to be transformed into something more than we have been—without losing our core identity—to accomplish the mission we have been called to.[2]

## The Pursuit to Follow Christ

Pursuing continual transformation should be evident for Jesus's people in the church. Sometimes people are just going through the motions by showing up unchanged and checking the boxes of those who are present, bring their Bibles, give, attend worship, and serve in some way. You may remember when items like this were asked of each person and filled out on attendance records for the church. We often reflect a well-managed and efficient people but not a highly transformed Christlike people. The organization needs to be efficient so its people are ministered to, but efficiency should not replace helping people reflect Christ. The "quiet time," as it has been labeled for Christians for decades, has traditionally been defined as Bible reading and prayer. The struggle for many is that this time is spent just reading and not really studying Scripture. According to the *State of the Bible Report*, only 19 percent of Americans stated that they read the Bible, with people from all generations pointing to limited time and many confessing that they were unsure where to start reading.[3] In light of this, the conversation between the senior adult ladies in the restaurant should not be surprising. Unfortunately, many people read other Christians' thoughts during their quiet time but do not

---

    [2] Tod Bolsinger, *Canoeing the Mountains* (Downers Grove, IL: IVP, 2015), 42.

    [3] "Newly Released—12th Annual State of the Bible Report: Scripture Reading Decreased Among Americans," *American Bible Society (blog),* April 6, 2022, https://news.americanbible .org/blog/entry/corporate-blog/newly-released-12th-annual-state-of-the-bible-report.

engage Scripture directly. These devotions usually have reasonable interpretations of Scripture and provide applications. The daily practice for those that have embraced these types of devotions will likely not have the "fluency required to understand and apply biblical teaching."[4] As people continue to live with little margin, their spiritual habits seem to be pushed aside or not included in their life rhythms. They may listen to the Bible app in the car or read over a devotional but will have little interaction with Scripture itself.

It is crucial for leaders to teach their people how to become devoted followers of Christ through spiritual habits and engage with them through their weekly schedules. As team members prepare to teach, interact with resources, and engage with the curriculum, they will have better skill sets and fluency to interact with the Scriptures to share with others. If the staff, both paid and volunteer, are lacking in their weekly devotion to the Lord, then it is likely that their preparation for leading in areas of ministry each week should be better. Serving through a ministry assignment or staff position does not replace the personal growth of a disciple but engages the disciple's development with practical hands-on experience in ministry. The two should work together for the holistic development of the person. If you randomly polled how many people spent devoted time in prayer during the week before serving, what would the response be on average: Fifteen minutes, thirty minutes, or seven hours of prayer during the week?

Suppose you were to take time and reflect on the moments when God moved in your life. A season that comes to mind was when I was in high school, where God moved powerfully over an issue. Sometimes to move forward, we must be reminded of our faithful God and how he has brought us this far. Even during the season of working on this book, there have been moments when God brought an idea or experience to memory that advised my writing as I prayed over the process. After years of ministry and several degrees, it is even more apparent I need to walk with him each day because I cannot do it on my own. Your ministry team needs that level of transparency so they know the struggle is not unique and that we all need personal development and devotion to the one who gave it all. Jesus modeled spiritual habits as he led in ministry, evident in the time he spent with the Father through

---

⁴ Dru Johnson and Celina Durgin, "Is It Time to Quit Quiet Time?" *Christianity Today,* March 13, 2023, https://christianitytoday.com/ct/2023/april/quit-quiet-time-devotions-bible -literacy-reading-scripture.html.

prayer. The spiritual habit that Jesus modeled the most was prayer. As I talk with leaders, this is often their weakest among the disciplines and the most needed to have more profound devotion with the Lord.

## Toil of Ministry

Ministry takes a toll on the volunteer lay leader and the ministerial staff. Burnout through serving is a common issue within the church. Healthy habits for a personal life of devotion are crucial to doing our God-given tasks well. A few key areas of self-discipline could be helpful for ministry service. Time stewardship, sleep, exercise, mental stability, and emotional control are all areas that doctors ask about as they try to discern the overall balance of life. God was the first to address these concerns: "Love the Lord your God with all your heart, with all your soul, with all your strength, and with all your mind; and your neighbor as yourself."[5] The need to prioritize emotional, spiritual, physical, and mental health in the overall development of a disciple requires an ongoing commitment to prioritizing these.

Several factors impact health, but two critical components are sleep and diet. You have interacted with grumpy people because they do not get enough rest. The Sabbath was introduced for people to have downtime. Technology has affected the ability of people to find rest. We have heard over the years that breakfast is the most important meal of the day or that you are what you eat. Researchers have different views on breakfast and diet, but the critical insight for people should be a healthy balanced diet. Many people push themselves beyond their limits by staying up late and skipping meals, just trying to get everything done. This only lasts for a season before people become tired, hungry, angry, or lonely:

> God gives us the grace and power to have a relationship with him. His word instructs us to run this race of faith. God's power is key to any transformational change in our lives, including our health. He wants us to plug into that power so we can live and move the way he intended…For too many of us, unhealthy choices have left us without the mental, physical, or spiritual energy to embrace what God has put us on this planet to do.[6]

  [5] Luke 10:27.
  [6] Rick Warren, Daniel Amen, and Mark Hyman, *The Daniel Plan: 40 Days to a Healthier Life* (Grand Rapids: Zondervan, 2013), 32–33.

# Church Culture of Health

The environment is vital to a development plan to live healthier for God's glory. If you have ever gardened, then you know the right soil conditions, amount of water, and hours of sunlight determine overall results. You can craft an overall health management plan as you decide on the growing need and intended outcomes of your church ministries. Challenges can arise with people in any church and distract ministers and volunteers from growing their relationships with Christ. Walking in unity is crucial to spiritual development. Suitable environments for practicing spiritual habits and cultivating a culture of accountability and admonishment can develop a health community. Ministry cannot be accomplished alone. As ministry leaders walk with Christ, the relationships around them should naturally strengthen. Accountability from a small close group of trustworthy people helps your ministers and volunteers become more like Christ.

A simple verse that reminds disciples of the overall need to grow in relationship with Christ is Mic 6:8. The Lord requires that we "Act justly." What do you think acting justly looks like in your life? We should be a people that is fair with one another in our dealings as we live out an ethic of right and wrong in all that we say and do. Loving mercy is an easier task, but how to apply loving mercy is a challenge. Recognizing the need for mercy from others does not always translate into living a life that is naturally merciful to people. Many aspects of life challenge people, from customer service issues to feelings of entitlement; the compassionate response of showing mercy to others is the challenge. Walking humbly can be a challenge as the cultural standard is driven by self-centeredness. As we serve from a humble position, people see disciples walking humbly.

Many people who continue to give through serving and helping others could be better at self-care. Establish time in your weekly calendar to be alone and not distracted to spend at least one hour with the Lord. Grab a Bible, pen, and notebook. Leave your phone in another room; remove distractions and find time to reflect, listen, and hear from the One you serve. You may not feel that you have an hour to avoid handling something or managing another issue, but this is a necessary rhythm in your workflow and time management that will become a refreshing time you will cherish. You will always have another email to send, post to make, or a text to answer, so carve out the time to be mindful of the work of the Lord in your life.

# Personal Management

Personal management and development in ministry can be hard to quantify, but consider a few items. Online opportunities to attend a conference virtually or download a video to learn a new skill or area of ministry has changed the landscape of personal development. Having an all-day conference or attending a workshop still has value, especially by debriefing what you have learned later. However, ministry leaders have options for ongoing resources to enhance their skills.

Personal management is the stewardship of becoming more like Christ, not just more efficient with job skills or people. Relationships are the connection between people in the church that should move to a deeper devotion collectively. As a leader, you must cultivate a deeper relationship with people on your team so you and your team can grow deeper. We see Jesus doing this among the disciples. Likewise, Paul mentored church leaders as they did ministry together. Peter instructed and led people in the church. You should be able to name people who have devoted time cultivating you into the leader God has called you to be. Reading certain Scripture might cause you to remember the instruction of a mentor. As you review a prayer journal from prior years, the influence of those devoted to the faith are evident in your life.

Family is one factor that ministry leaders must devote attention to and develop. The church should not get all the focus of a minister's time and margin, resulting in the family being pushed aside. If you are married, your spouse needs that relationship nurtured. If you have children, they need to know you care to devote your attention and develop them into what God has called them to be. Dane Ortlund reminds parents, "Our job is to show our kids that even our best love is a shadow of a greater love. To put a sharper edge on it: to make the tender heart of Christ irresistible and unforgettable. Our goal is that our kids would leave the house at eighteen and be unable to live the rest of their lives believing that their sins and sufferings repel Christ."[7]

The devotion to cultivating others not just for a position but to walk with Christ is vital to the kingdom and the disciples around you. The responsibility of a leader is to reflect the holiness of God and be an example for others to follow Jesus more deeply. Devotion to the Lord is sometimes siloed, which is part of the personal relationship of

---

[7] Dane Ortlund, *Gentle and Lowly: The Heart of Christ for Sinners and Sufferers* (Wheaton, IL: Crossway, 2020), 100.

walking with Christ. However, that devotion must also be publicized in managing the congregation. As we age, the lens from which our perspective is viewed will need to be considered as we develop people. Cultivating lifelong learners that serve the Lord in a healthy pattern of devotion and development follows Paul's charge to Timothy: "You, therefore, my son, be strong in the grace that is in Christ Jesus. What you have heard from me in the presence of many witnesses, commit to faithful men who will be able to teach others also."[8] Commit to devoting yourself to walking with the Lord daily, cultivate your relationships, including your family, and entrust others to be devoted to the faith that will continue to develop others.

A word of caution should be noted here. Serving the church is not a suitable replacement for walking with Christ. As a ministry leader, cultivating a daily journey with spiritual practices, habits, and routines should inform your service. On any given day, the struggles of this life continually vie for attention and devotion; we must deny those and follow Christ. Jesus was tempted forty days and forty nights, and he was hungry. The tempter questioned every aspect of Jesus's identity and even challenged whether he could change the circumstances. We face the same tempter who knows everything about us and desires to call out who we are and what our struggles are that challenges our will to live for Christ.

James encourages us as we face various challenges with these words: "Consider it a great joy, my brothers and sisters, whenever you experience various trials, because you know that the testing of your faith produces endurance. And let endurance have its full effect, so that you may be mature and complete, lacking nothing."[9]

Based on Jesus's temptation, he knows what we face, and we can reach out to him if we struggle through life's challenges. Every Christian will face times of struggle, which will evidence itself through the church. People share their joys, struggles, and even things they do not like. Personal devotion is vital to the church being unified as people struggle. In a congregation, people will not struggle with or experience the same issues simultaneously, and leaders will need to shepherd their churches through trials, helping people develop endurance through their challenges.

---

[8] 2 Tim 2:1–2.

[9] Jas 1:2–4.

### Questions to Consider

1. Who has invested in your life? Create a list. Send them a note thanking them.
2. To whom are you investing your life? Create a list. Develop a management plan to invest in their life.
3. Who in your ministry does not have someone investing in their lives? Create an investment plan for your people.

## Chapter 14:

# Changing Approaches toward Church and Attendance

People in previous generations could not conceive of the conveniences that many enjoy today around the world, such as apps that allow same-day or next-day delivery to the door. The smartphone has replaced the landline luxury for the wealthy, and is now a standard device utilized by millions worldwide. Since writing letters has evolved into emails and now text messages, it is within reason to wonder what will change in church attendance. A senior adult trip I led to Ohio's Amish country revealed a primitive way of doing church. They allowed us to join a worship service in a home where we enjoyed a meal. They had all the supplies to convert a living and dining room into a worship center. The pulpit, benches, and hymnals were the essential tools for their church to meet and function. Many churches in the past had a more basic structure with no technology. Today, however, most churches have modernized to include air conditioning, sound systems, and technology that enhances their time together.

Virtual meetings, online classes, and remote learning caused the educational world to pivot during the COVID-19 pandemic utilizing technology in ways not considered previously and requiring people to learn new ways of working and learning. Adapting to the technological world has caused many people to be more open to connecting and doing life through technology. The struggle has been to balance new approaches alongside the tradition of cherished structure. Many families learned to share life milestones through video calls when travel was not an option to be together for a birthday or Christmas gathering. As generations of all ages have been using technology in more ways than ever, various church attendance approaches have increased. Facebook became a common way for churches of all sizes to stream their services to a larger audience. As the methods morphed quickly with technology and a necessity to keep people engaged with opportunities to gather and be connected, the philosophy toward a digital option became mainstream for the local church.

Virtual options are now offered from the smallest to the largest church for people to connect from anywhere. The possibility of being connected though not physically in the room previously emerged when larger churches began simulcasting to other campuses. A minister was assigned to each location to support and engage the participants at a distance or step up and speak if the technology failed. Various models for multisite services or campuses have emerged in recent years to allow churches to expand their reach from one location. Although pastors of various sizes have decried this model, the internet, social media apps, and smartphones have allowed any size congregation with these three options to stream their services as a multisite model worldwide. Many churches of all sizes rushed to virtual options during the pandemic because the spread of COVID-19 prevented churches from hosting live gatherings. Changing opportunities for people has thus created a shift in the approach people take toward their attendance and volunteerism through church ministries.

Social media has caused ministry leaders to be more aware of what another church, pastor, or ministry is doing to attract people or engage in ministry. The struggle with this new level of knowledge is that much time is spent pondering what others are doing than meditating over what needs to happen in the context one is already serving. Over the years, people have been aware of what others were doing in ministry through conferences, letters, and conversations, but not to the extent of seeing and reading about other people and their churches throughout the day. This level of knowledge has led to a culture questioning whether a church will be relevant if it does not pivot and utilize a new technology, marketing strategy, or method. As a professor and pastor, I want to be continually learning. My passion is to sharpen my skills and increase my knowledge in all areas of life and ministry. I will add a word of caution, however, we were not designed to constantly interpret the massive level of ongoing online information that actually distracts us more than it engages us to excel in ministry. The challenge for you as a leader is to discern how much social media, podcasts, and inbox information for a new method, idea, or concept for doing ministry is healthy for your development as a leader. Take some time and reflect on how much information concerning ministry options and methods your congregation needs before it also overwhelms them.

The bigger question about the various digital options is whether there is a biblical foundation for the digital opportunity. The Bible speaks of the believers gathering together. The building and methods for gathering have changed over the centuries from homes to cathedrals. The music and programs have also shifted with culture and time as people of the nations have different styles of music and options for buildings to gather for worship. The shifts are happening, and people will continue to debate methods as we adapt to various technologies and cultural themes that impact our styles and preferences. My travels have taken me to worship in Central America, Europe, the Middle East, and across America. The ability to worship the one true God is possible through various styles and strategies whether in cathedrals, block buildings, large state-of-the-art rooms, or old pews in a sanctuary. Approaches are strategies to enable people to worship and gather together as the church. Access to the internet with smartphones, televisions, and computers has allowed people across the nations to have a new option to gather.

People were hesitant about the phone, television, and the internet, but all three are now everyday aspects of life. If I missed church as a kid because of sickness, my mom would teach the Sunday School lesson to me, and we would watch a worship service on our console television. We made cassettes, CDs, VHS, and DVDs for shut-ins or those that missed worship each week for decades until the technology emerged to stream a service anytime from the church. The "tape ministry," as it was labeled, ministered to thousands that missed worship services over the years due to health, work, or vacation. Tape ministry could be argued to be a form of virtual options to participate or view the services today. Digital or multimedia choices have paved the way to make it possible for streaming options today.

## Navigating Virtual Options

The struggle with virtual options is when streaming worship is the only way a person chooses to connect with the local church. They have limited or no options to utilize their gifts within the church, which is a challenge to resolve. After speaking at a conference, a minister shared with me that a couple who lived over 1,000 miles away joined their church, connected to a small group via ZOOM with some of their friends from years ago, and attended worship online. You may have heard the phrase, "A church alive is worth the drive," but a new saying might be, "The stream is worth the view if the dream is clicked." This might be a stretch for some people. The reach of the local church is now regional and, for some, global due to internet options. This requires churches to consider how to connect with virtual guests and members. As younger generations adapt and create new media platforms, this conversation of virtual interaction and attendance is in the infancy stage. Artificial intelligence will change the options to an unimaginable level.

Challenges, adaptations, and new opportunities become apparent whenever a new model or option is introduced. Finding new means to connect with people by creating opportunities to engage with some the church may never have connected with in the first place. These opportunities can only be realized to their potential if church leaders develop a strategy for utilizing online apps and other digital connectivity.

How can churches track connection and community? Loss of interaction and loss of awareness of people's lives and concerns make it easy to fade into the shadows. The ability to be present but not have to interact is attractive for some people. Families that struggle to get ready and out the door can have a less hurried morning. The struggle is not over convenience but rather adapting to technology in the culture. Since churches have introduced the technology on-site and as a means to connect to people during a pandemic, the various groups that utilize the option are not limited to one age. Shut-ins and elderly that cannot come, retirees traveling, grandparents visiting their grandkids, families traveling for sports and arts, and singles that desire to avoid being in a crowded room are just a few of the various people being more open to a distance option for worship.

## Changing Attendance Patterns

Inconsistent attendance is the more consistent pattern for many, but inconsistency may not mean that they are failing to connect. People may miss the in-person gathering and still choose to view the worship service during the week. Some may choose to move between congregations as they worship with family and friends connected to other churches. This is common for gyms, restaurants, and other businesses; the church is just another area where people are becoming more fluid in their loyalty. This can vary demographically. Some cities or regions have fewer churches, but people may still choose to have online options that speak into their lives. Tracking metrics for how people connect with the church and through its ministries will be essential as people are more fluid in their attendance.[1]

People may choose to go between options. A person may be at the beach, traveling for work, caring for family, or just tired or sick. Innovation is not always easy to implement even when it provides more options. Weekly preparation and hard work were needed for previous innovations of television ministries or duplicating videos for shut-ins. The challenge for changing options becomes how to staff these ministries differently based on changing attendance patterns. If you have guests online, how do you capture people not physically in the room? How do you cultivate staying connected with those attending virtually? Do you restructure the staff to have direct ministerial oversight of virtual options? What is the process for deciding whether an event can have more than a physical in-person option? Here are a few ideas to help you capture your thoughts on these questions. Assign a volunteer greeter ministry to monitor online viewers. Have volunteer hosts that interact with people and offer the same level of support as in-person gatherings. Shepherd online attendance with the same level of pastoral care as in-person worship.

The effort to get out of bed, get ready, and travel to the physical building is a different experience than logging into a worship service

---

[1] Aaron Earls, "5 Current Church Attendance Trends You Need to Know," *Lifeway Research*, February 2, 2022, https://research.lifeway.com/2022/02/02/5-current-church-attendance-trends -you-need-to-know/.

or small group remotely. If the alternative is skipping a week not to attend at all, virtual is better, but it is not an equivalent experience for most. Larger churches have more options than a smaller rural church can achieve for attendance options.

Discipline, sacrifice, and effort are words repeated frequently by leadership in the church over the years regarding attending and serving within the local church. Churches in the past met more than most do today, but these aspects must be considered in the discussion. Discipline in attendance is part of commitment to a local church. The challenge with virtual delivery is that it offers many options for various preaching styles and types of ministries without the commitment to one local body of believers. Sacrifice is the concept that a person makes an intentional choice not to expect convenience but rather make a commitment that costs something to be a part of through time, energy, service, and participation. I am disciplined to go to church and choose to sacrifice my conveniences by staying committed. Is the effort involved in committing to a local church vital to your walk with and service unto the Lord?

Churches have been morphing in their construction and conduct since the early church days. A local body of believers gathered in a village hut, a rented gym at a school, or an excellent facility designed for worship have aspects in common. However, churches worldwide have different challenges with shifts in attendance. American churches have rapidly decreasing attendance. Research by the Barna Group states that average worship attendance is declining as people become more private about spiritual faith.[2] Sunday evening church was a shift in practice during agriculture time to allow people more time to gather their crops before worship.[3] Changing the schedule to accommodate people's needs is one aspect that changes the tone of the debate. Modern American culture no longer has a blue law where businesses close early on Wednesdays or close completely on Sundays. The approach to the shifts in attendance indicates the need to be aware of what people need in light of their work to be able to participate. We have a more seven-day-a-week lifestyle and work system. Some people work

[2] Barna Group, "Year in Review: Barna's Top 10 Releases of 2022," *Barna*, December 21, 2022, https://www.barna.com/research/year-in-review-2022/.

[3] Thom S. Rainer, "Whatever Happened to Sunday Evening Services?" *Church Answers (blog)*, May 10, 2014, https://churchanswers.com/blog/whatever-happened-sunday-evening-services/.

weekends only, have a shift schedule, or travel, which causes Sunday morning not to be the time slot when almost everyone is available.

## Changing Life Patterns

Due to work and life schedules, gathering for multiple services and days of the week beyond Sundays has been a shared philosophy for churches for decades. In the past, churches in the rural areas of America would move worship for crop gatherings during harvest times. Challenges to weekly schedules today result from a constantly working society that is always on the move, with family, leisure, sports, and work schedules varied across the ages.

The overall patterns of the church in the Western world are shifting in many ways due to cultural customs from a pandemic, rising social unrest, and political divides. Children are one aspect of the changing patterns of the church. The Gen Z generation has been raised in a connected society. On a recent birthday, my son created a "blooket" about himself to play for the family. At his school, each student has an iPad issued to them, and they create these blooklets as they review classwork. This was a natural, free time creation he decided to do for his birthday. Church is the one place where he is completely unplugged from anything digital when he sits beside us in worship. When considering changing patterns, we can easily rationalize that church for centuries has been primarily an oral tradition. We can further our stance by stating how worship is conducted. As streaming and a constantly digitally connected culture continue to develop, methods should be pondered. Could children be connected through an app to keep them engaged in worship?

Considering digital individual participation options may seem unthinkable. However, adults eventually installed telephones, running water, electricity, cable television, and high-speed internet. Many attend worship each week with a smartphone in their pocket or purse. More and more pastors use tablets instead of printed copies of the Bible as they preach. Worship services have more digital aspects to them, no matter the size of the church. As society over the past hundred years has seen a constant morphing with options for modern conveniences like running water, indoor restrooms, and climate control, the digital developments cause us to have similar conversations that many older adults in the church previously had to consider. The church has continued to change since the first gathering as civilization has adapted to the ingenuity of people to create and build all around us. So, we ask what we can utilize for Christ and his church to continue to advance the Gospel and make disciples.

## New Trends Toward Church

Emerging trends or shifts in philosophy in the church have ebbed and flowed over time. America's church history is a relatively short time in the history of the global church. The foundations with which we exist currently once emerged from a trend or shift in philosophy in the past. These were sometimes needed and well-founded for the church's expansion or clarification of doctrine. The recent changes in how the church meets or be accessible to individual congregants is a tiny spec on the timeline of the church Jesus commended to Peter. These trends should not be because of popularity, cultural shifts, or membership preferences. New models should emerge because a biblical foundation allows for a tweak in style or delivery. The trends should be founded on correcting a former model that has strayed from the original intent.

One current trend is a correction to many congregations that have chosen ethnicity preferences or exclusivity instead of a biblical foundation of the local church reflecting the community. A church design where the Gospel is available to everyone in the community is a biblical portrait of the local church. In Acts 1:8, Jesus sent the early church disciples to minister within their community to move beyond their region and ultimately reach the nations. As American churches consider diversity, this is not a tweak to inclusiveness where lifestyle choices or cultural trends impact the church methods but a shift in culture that welcomes each person created by God and invites people to be a part of the total membership. Diversity does not mean culturally relevant or politically correct but reflecting the church God intended where everyone in a community is invited to hear the Gospel, respond to the invitation, join in worship, and be discipled. This is a sensitive topic in our churches and among ministry leaders of different ethnicities, various church sizes, and denominations. The question that each church needs to ask is whether the composition of the congregation reflects the composition of the community. If your church does not reflect the community, then what could you do to reach your community through the emerging trends you employ for ministry? Peter reminds us to be hospitable to others. What does that mean for us in our community with a diverse make up of people? Hospitality to others, even in virtual communication, is part of being a good neighbor.

Another issue that we are observing is the impact of burnout. Older people have lived during times of difficulty that seemed worse because of the physical demand of that season. The mental demand of today causes people to desire downtime because they are digitally overwhelmed and exhausted. Studies are beginning to reveal this impact on young people and adults. The unseen mental health effects of online connectivity cause people to shift their involvement in public life. This challenge gives us ministry opportunities to help people. Consider the COVID-19 pandemic and the rapid innovation of churches for calling people, FM radio in the parking lot, and streaming services. Innovation is not on the radar every week for the membership, but the pandemic caused many to innovate and be flexible over the desire to return to some form of normalcy. Worship was one aspect people quickly missed and desired to find some way to make happen. Socially-distanced choirs, formalized seating patterns, extra services, and offerings collected in various ways were all changes congregants were typically willing to accept. A horrific pandemic created a short season of innovation for many churches with an openness to trying new methods. People did quickly pivot back to their former customs and traditions once the season was over, but some aspects of their innovation have remained.

Feeding people without a potluck or creating social distancing events were foreign concepts for many churches pre-pandemic. Church staff members had yet to contemplate many aspects of their innovative ideas. FM transmitters to have a parking lot service where people remained in their vehicles was a common idea to gather for worship—it almost resembled an old drive-in. Churches without installed video equipment learned to utilize their smartphones for Facebook Live. Some of these options were not ideal or long-term but were innovative for the time. With this same mindset, people in churches should consider ongoing innovation for ministries and the church.

Adaptation that leads to adoption is a struggle for people. We adapt to our surroundings or work within the framework to function as it relates to our current conditions. You may adapt to meeting in the gym or fellowship hall for a sanctuary remodel. Weeks of inconvenience causes the congregation to adapt to new surroundings and conditions but with the hope of going back to previous methods. Adoption is a different perspective because we decide to follow the church's leader-ship or adopt a new way of doing ministry or even the willingness to make someone else's method our method for ministry. People are more willing to adapt than adopt innovative leadership and methods in the church. This struggle is an ongoing tension of various ages and experiences and can cause resistance in unexpected ways. Spiritual growth through the work of the Holy Spirit can enable us to adapt and adopt quickly to what God is leading the church to do. As we reflect on the early church, we see people change at a moment's notice and not only adapt to their surroundings but adopt the methods of those around them. We also see people that struggle to adapt or adopt to the ministry and theological practices of others. This ongoing process of adapting and adopting can cause us to be weary in ministry, but we are encour-aged by Paul's exhortations to stay focused and serve faithfully. This process teaches us that God directs our path and steps, and we will have to adopt his will for our lives and ministries and not cling to our own, which should be reflected through how we serve the church. We should incorporate into our lives and ministry rhythms the practices and means the Lord leads us toward. As a church, you are probably an incorporated organization, meaning at some point in the church's history, the people covenanted together to exist as a whole and not as individual people.

### Questions to Consider

1.  How willing are you to adopt the ways of the Lord into your life?
2.  What changes should your church make to its announcements, information sharing, and options given? (Review your wor-ship guides, screens, marketing, and spoken announcements.)
3.  What is your approach to connecting with those that attend online?

## Chapter 15:

# Streamlining the Work and Organization

M eet Taylor, a devoted staff member everyone loves and is always available, but no one can pinpoint exactly what she does or what her job is supposed to look like. The former pastor hired her and people are unsure where she fits in the new structure. Jacob has been the worship pastor for several years, and everyone loves his demeanor, ability to lead the congregation in worship, and ability with technology. He works about twenty-five to thirty hours per week, but he does not desire to do pastoral care ministry. People in the congregation believe the church is too large to streamline its full-time staff roles, but several full-time positions no longer have the same full-time responsibilities.

In another church, Stephen is a bi-vocational minister and would love to become full-time. The church is pondering combining several part-time positions into one full-time position for him. Fewer staff members could streamline the staffing structure but would reduce diversity of voices, experiences, and views on the team. Streamlining should have a process for weighing the options for overall organizational health. More holes become apparent when one person is absent.

One person cannot be in two places simultaneously, so in the organization, people must understand the change if roles are combined. Streamlining has worked in organizations that chose this path for their staff and overall work. Volunteers are critical to successfully integrate the roles into one position, and different ministry areas will need volunteers to help fill gaps as they occur.

Another church has many volunteer roles that are no longer needed in the church, but people are attached to ministry programs, traditions, or their control over an aspect of the church. Jeff Iorg states that change is hard because it "is the new circumstances introduced into organizational life. Transition, on the other hand, is the emotional, psychological, and spiritual adjustments people go through when change is implemented."[1] Streamlining the work means transitioning the church to embrace a more straightforward approach. To analyze the people and their roles, property and its function, finances and their expenses, programs and their effectiveness, and processes and their simplicity, a leader or a team must be willing to consider the organization from the lens of greater effectiveness.

The word *streamlining* has been used in business to motivate a workforce to consider how to utilize operations more efficiently. A simple definition for streamlining is "to streamline an organization or process to make it more efficient by removing unnecessary parts of it."[2] Many may think that discipleship, worship, prayer, or fellowship cannot be simplified. In the post-pandemic world, exhaustion, mental health, and the ultimate desire to live a simpler existence continue as people strive to streamline their lives to find margin. Several years ago, a book was introduced that caused many ministers to take a pause and consider two words: "simple church." Thom S. Rainer and Eric Geiger concluded after hundreds of consultations with local churches that many leaders in the local church desired to simplify. They found these leaders asking two questions: "How can we make all this work, and how can we put all the pieces together?"[3] Several decades later, the same questions continue to be asked, as churches struggle not to simply repeat the calendar each year and exhaust already tired members. As you consider your work and your organization, begin to ponder if you have days, events, processes, or aspects that could be streamlined.

---

[1] Jeff Iorg, *Leading Major Change in Your Ministry* (Nashville: B&H, 2018), 53.
[2] https://www.collinsdictionary.com/us/dictionary/english/streamline.
[3] Thom S. Rainer and Eric Geiger, *Simple Church* (Nashville: B&H, 2006), 4.

In a previous chapter, we discussed solutions to our collective organizational work. This chapter will look beyond the work of the organization to ways to streamline work, simplify processes, and create leaner organizational practices.

Simplicity, streamline, and success are words that appear in books across the spectrum of personal health, business, and ministry. People want to simplify approaches to their personal lives and in their work. As society moves forward, people desire simplicity in ministry. Streamlining ministry or the church for efficiency and productivity seems like a reasonable proposition. Success is a factor that families even use to compare how well their kids perform academically or in sports. The metrics for success are fluid for those in the church based on their expectations and life experiences. You can refer to chapter seven on metrics for further reflection, but for the streamlining factors, the metrics and processes will need to be revised as one simplifies the organization.

Each aspect of society has published resources addressing living a simpler existence. In business, the concept of streamlining is for increasing production or improving the bottom line. In management around the assembly line, the idea of quota was introduced to increase production. In retail, numbers are tracked by employers to increase the daily sales by working with each floor salesperson to increase their contact with customers. For years, the car industry has had daily sales goals and different metrics for tracking those contacts, points of contact, and closed deals. The stress of succeeding has trickled into academics at all ages, from preschool to doctoral programs. The workforce has long been dealing with the stress of streamlining their work to be more efficient. A drive for more has even been in the church as pastors scan the crowd in worship, count cars in the parking lot, or track offerings. The struggle caused people to question whether they can do more with less. This could mean working with fewer employees, less income, or less space. Sometimes, the struggle to get everything done week in and week out causes many to ponder if it has to be this way.

## Retirement and Transition in the Workforce

The American church is having to deal with a large swath of the workforce entering their retirement season of life. Volunteers and paid staff in the church are aging, and the immediate generation behind them

include fewer people with less interest in serving as their predecessors
served the church. If you have fewer people or more retired people,
then the work of streamlining becomes a necessity. A shrinking workforce has created several challenges that have been addressed, but one
remaining factor is how to achieve the mission with less. Transitions
are hard on people as they force organizational change. The transition
of a staff member, a ministry program, or lay volunteers can naturally
create the opportunity to streamline the work. Roger Parrott reminds
Christian leaders to "spend more time dreaming, praying, and listen-
ing to what God wants for us, rather than huddled around conference
tables attempting to plan God's best for us...Operational, localized
planning is vital to a well-managed ministry. But putting too much
energy into planning an unknown future will drain the life from your
ministry."[4]

Organizations tend to believe their model has to stay the same
as they simply replace vacancies. Younger generations entering the
workforce desire to contribute and will bring new ideas, dreams, and
methods into the work. Older generations worry about the cost and
will ask if the current model is affordable. Motivations for streamlining the work come from different angles and require the leadership to
understand what needs to be accomplished. Once needs are clarified,
the result can be refined to a new model for a leaner system. Iorg has
led churches, a state convention, and a seminary through significant
changes that, in many ways, streamlined the work toward fulfilling
their mission. His perspective on leading significant change to leverage people, property, and finances toward God's mission is captivating:

> God's glory—achieved through advancing his kingdom—must be
> the ultimate end of every major change. Do not get bogged down
> or sidetracked by lesser motives. They will frustrate your leadership
> and demotivate your followers. Focus on the ultimate objective—
> people transformed into a diverse, global community for God's eter-
> nal companionship. With that end in view, major change becomes a
> joyful, obedient step in the right direction on the adventure of doing
> ministry in the twenty-first century.[5]

[4] Roger Parrott, *The Longview: Lasting Strategies for Rising Leaders,* (Colorado Springs:
David C. Cook, 2009), 151.
[5] Iorg, *Leading Major Change,* 182–83.

## Reconsidering the Process

Complexity should never be the goal of a congregation. Some churches have systems in which the work is complicated, and pastors and ministry leaders struggle to lead and serve in such a system. For example, a congregational process might include a committee passing its work to another committee, followed by questions that cause the second committee to pass the work back to the first committee. Ninety days later, the decision is moved to the deacon's meeting, where questions arise that are then referred to the original committee. After 150 days of back and forth with staff, committees, and deacons, a motion is ready to present in a congregational business meeting. The church has questions and tables the motion from the committee until the next business meeting. One hundred eighty days later after two business meetings, the process is now approved, and the ministry can move forward. This example shows why younger generations may not understand how simple ministry decisions and ideas to move the church forward can somehow take half a year to approve.

A complicated bureaucratic process was not the intent of congregational church polity. You may ask what church polity has to do with streamlining our collective work. According to Chad Owen Brand and R. Stanton Norman, "Church polity is the manner in which a church or denomination practices organization and governance. Because these two principles permeate all areas of church life, polity has profound implications for understanding the nature of the church and its various functions and ministries."[6] Polity determines the approach ministry teams can take to streamline their work. Many people in ministry become bogged down with administrative tasks. They would like to simplify the process, but some factors inhibit their ability work within the organization's structure. Brand and Norman pointed out, polity has implications for various functions and ministries, which can translate to any of the options for church governance.[7] One needed component when considering a streamlined approach with technology and polity is what can be worked through a congregationally involved process in a shorter time with streamlined procedures.

---

[6] Chad Owen Brand and R. Stanton Norman, ed. *Perspectives on Church Government: Five Views of Church Polity* (Nashville: B&H Academic, 2004), 5.

[7] Brand and Norman, *Perspectives on Church Government*, 5.

Pastor-led, ministry-minded, and congregationally-informed is the process for a congregational polity structure. Voting slows down the process and creates challenges as people desire a simplified process and structure. Business meetings, committee processes, and leadership challenges do not excite most people. Adults often try to avoid staff meetings, dodge being asked to serve on committees outside of the church, and steer clear of relationship difficulties. Streamlining processes and structures is needed because people desire to spend less time in meetings and focus more of their energy on developing their community. The dysfunctional aspects of committee structures thrive off conflict to reach decisions, while a healthy solution for some adults differs from how younger generations desire to invest their time. The political divide in America has caused people to think that disagreement means that someone is against them. These issues are all more difficult as more generations are involved in leadership in the church. The various perspectives brought to the table cause change and can be stressful or complex.

## Systems and Structures that Simplify

Some churches still operate with limited digital options and overburden people with administrative ministry structures. Many churches have moved toward a digital influence, with many aspects of their work communicated through apps, emails, and group text messages. Every church must find an approach to streamline their work as fewer people are willing to give a lot of time each week to volunteer. Another factor to streamlining is a lack of clearly defined boundaries, where everything competes for people's time and attention. The church is the place that is getting the most pressure to have streamlined solutions to function effectively. Ministry needs are greater than ever, so less time can be devoted to organizational management factors.

Cohesive systems throughout the organization are vital to the overall organizational health. If you can develop a streamlined approach to your management process with people, property, finance, and programming, then time is freed up to invest in coaching and have margin for challenges. Streamlining your organization involves intentionally recalibrating your processes so that your structure is simple enough for volunteers, support workers, and staff members to understand. Although a reset and developing new foundations will take time, your focus can pivot to manage the work. This margin allows people the freedom to lead and develop their areas of responsibility.

As time passes without an intentional recalibration, organizations become more complex. The challenges create isolation, hesitancy toward change, and a constant addition of new ideas without eliminating old ones. Complexity can cause people to become frustrated, disengaged, or overwhelmed in their involvement. A simpler time of no electricity, no full-time staff, limited resources, and less structure may seem appealing, but every iteration of the church has had its challenges. Leading people to think about simpler ways of achieving the work and recalibrating when needed creates a more efficient organization. An intriguing book on simplifying the church entitled *Deliberate Simplicity* causes the reader to reevaluate the complexities of the modern church: "A scalable church needs transferable ideals, clear descriptions, repeatable procedures, disseminated information, and a supportive structure."[8] When considering your organizational structure, systems, and methods, does simplicity arise as a chief concern? This is not the first time the church has considered how to simplify, transfer knowledge to the younger generation, or transition to a new phase of ministry as a church.

*Faithful* is a word that should describe streamlining in an organization. Leaders should not be deterred by the function or difficulty of the organization. Some may have life experiences that foster more efficient processes for the work. People are not always open to new methods, but developing and managing the organization to keep a streamlined approach is essential for ongoing ministry: "Streamlining is the process used to simplify or eliminate unnecessary work-related tasks to improve the efficiency of processes in businesses or organizations. Streamlining processes require the usage of modernizing techniques, technology, and other possible approaches to complete."[9] Streamlining an aspect of the church does not mean that the way you have been doing something is wrong. The process is designed to help the church improve. This is a common practice in businesses and organizations to continue forward in a healthy manner. Every region has unique ways of doing ministry. Your streamlined

[8] Dave Browning, *Deliberate Simplicity* (Grand Rapids: Zondervan, 2009), 185.
[9] Indeed Editorial Team, "6 Ways to Streamline Business Processes and Workflows," *Indeed,* last updated March 11, 2023, https://www.indeed.com/career-advice/career-development/streamline-processes-and-workflows.

process may not be the same for another culture or even another congregation that works with the same impact.

One of my favorite verses over the years has been, "Therefore, my dear brothers and sisters, be steadfast, immovable, always excelling in the Lord's work, because you know that your labor is not in vain."[10] *Steadfast* describes people who do not waver in their work but are trusted and faithful. They model for leaders the immovable nature of being firmly rooted in biblical convictions. Excellent leaders are simply those who are dependable throughout their ministry. These are the types of leaders you need on your team to walk through a streamlining process for managing the organization effectively.

If you conduct a simple search on the internet, you can find articles on streamlining maintenance, programs, processes, human resource challenges, worship services, staff meetings, and online services. This topic is now a common consideration among church leaders. The process of adjusting and streamlining the work can be tackled from two paths. First, you examine the whole organization from top to bottom and simplify each aspect or area. This is a radical step to tackle a total organizational makeover and might be more than your people can handle. The second path is to streamline area by area, beginning with an exhaustive list. Prioritize and focus on one area at a time until each area has a streamlined process to work more effectively for kingdom impact. Your organization may need to tackle property because deferred maintenance issues are at critical stages. Your programming may have taken over the organization, driving the work of the church instead of the overall mission. Alternatively, your church may have several areas with similar needs that can be tackled together for a simplified approach.

Although people want to accomplish more with less complexity, the desire to simplify must be balanced with essential and reasonable care for people, property, and the program processes of your organization. Remember your church serves in a changing society where new issues emerge every three to five years that merit reconsideration.

Essential skills needed in the organization, primary ministries, and opportunities to reach and make disciples should be the driving forces for your church. As these become a focus within the organization's DNA, business management through people, finances, property,

---

[10] 1 Cor 15:58.

and programs can be evaluated for how to streamline administrative functions in the church. As a leader, you may be tempted to observe how another organization functions and assume it is better. Although principles, processes, or practices can be transferred, they do not always streamline the work in your organization in the same way. A leader can sometimes influence how well the process functions, a principle is executed, or a practice is employed. Take the time to understand why it works better in another organization before trying to replicate it within your own. The value to the church when streamlining work is that when things function more efficiently, more resources are made available for developing those within the organization. The other added value is that people have more time and energy to reach and make disciples.

## Questions to Consider

1. Do your organization's guiding documents allow the leadership to make decisions during a crisis, emergency, or unforeseen national issue?

2. What structures can be suspended if circumstances prevent leadership teams, committees, or the congregation from having enough people with a quorum to conduct business?

3. If the polity of your organization is congregation confirmation for decisions but pastor-led, what leadership organizational structure is in place?

4. How does your organization define a quorum for digital meetings?

5. Does your organization provide live interactive video options for digital meetings or allow for viewing recorded business sessions or committee meetings?

6. Does your organization have digital records of meetings, minutes, and decisions to validate who, when, where, why, and how?

7. What areas of your organization could be simplified?

8. What are areas of frustration that hinder the work of your organization?

9. What procedures operate on people's preferences that could be simplified?

10. Generational differences can complicate agreement on streamlining approaches. What gaps exist among the generations in how to approach the work of the church?

# Conclusion

E ach church has opportunities to be more effective in their execution. It is a blessing to eat at a restaurant where the staff executes all elements of the experience well or to have an employee that goes above and beyond in a store to help with an issue. The same is true in the church when we can equip teams to administer the work well. Managing can be draining because it can place a leader into a posture of firefighting, as it seems there is always an issue smoldering somewhere. My hope is that as you have finished reading this resource, it has helped you in your ability to manage the work God has called you to lead.

In the next week, find a simple solution that you can tweak in one area. Begin to track the effect of these simple management changes. Over the next month, forecast areas in the administration that have immediate needs and create a ninety-day plan that can be executed. Look ahead to the next ninety days to a year or more for bigger issues or concerns that need attention, whether a process, financial aspect, or property improvement. As you begin to improve in these areas, ongoing administrative workflow will have a better rhythm. This fresh review of the work in the church and of yourself should also open a discussion of what you are doing well and what could be delegated to someone else on the team. Also consider aspects that could be discontinued or redesigned.

This guide for church administration is intended to provide information or instructions that will help you in your ministry setting. It is not a manual because specific instructions will depend on the size of the organization with varied applications. As a guide, it provides key information for foundational areas of church administration for you to consider. In addition, information was included for challenges that are constant and ongoing for a church of any size. The areas of coaching were intended to provide more information on how to invest in the church and each other to be better engaged.

"Be steadfast, immovable, always excelling in the Lord's work, because you know that your labor in the Lord's work is not in vain." This reminder from Paul in 1 Cor 15:58 reminds us that the focus of the work should be on him and for him. This has served as a life verse for me in the world of church administration. Management requires ongoing attention to details and can be exhausting. The administrative tasks of ministry should not overwhelm the spiritual tasks to the point the formation of ministry and people is lacking. Ongoing review of this practical guide can help you navigate management as needed.

Sometimes we like to tackle the biggest struggle first, but if you have ever started a new exercise routine, you know the end goal is not achieved the first day. As you begin to tackle areas of your ministry, develop an administrative plan to guide you with a metered approach to the tasks. At this point in your work, you know what is achievable based on your schedule. Develop your plan with tweaks that fit within your wheelhouse of work but also stretches you to improve. We utilize a similar approach in spiritual formation in helping a new believer begin to take on disciplines, actions, and pursuits to follow the Lord. You will need discipline in the administrative formation of your ongoing work. New action may be needed to help you manage at a higher level. A healthy pursuit could be nurtured through your ongoing work as you begin to focus on facing challenges from a spiritual work perspective.

A mentor can be an asset to navigating challenges or sharing victories as you manage the work in your ministry. Consider finding a mentor in ministry that can serve as a field guide in your administrative and discipleship pathways. This guide will help you as you implement or pivot in various areas in the church. The work is ongoing and needs leaders that lean in to cultivate a healthy administrative culture.

May you join with the thousands of people making it happen each week as you enhance the administrative ministry of your church.

# Name and Subject Index

# Scripture Index